FAMILIES HELPING FAMILIES

Living With Schizophrenia

FAMILIES HELPING FAMILIES

Living With Schizophrenia

by Families of the Mentally Ill Collective

Nona Dearth, *Chairman*
Barbara J. Labenski
M. Elizabeth Mott
Lillian M. Pellegrini

W · W · Norton & Company
New York   *London*

Published simultaneously in Canada by Penguin Books Canada Ltd, 2801 John Street, Markham, Ontario L3R 1B4

Printed in the United States of America.

This book is composed in Baskerville.
Composition and manufacturing by The Maple-Vail Book Group

Library of Congress Cataloging-in-Publication Data
Main entry under title:
Families helping families.
  Bibliography: p.
  1. Schizophrenics—Family relationships.
2. Schizophrenics—Home care. I. Dearth, Nona.
II. Families of the Mentally Ill Collective (Middlesex
County, Mass.) [DNLM: 1. Family. 2. Schizophrenia.
WM 203 F1956]
RC514.F324 1986   616.89'82   85–32082
ISBN 0-393-02301-X

ISBN 0-393-02301-X

W. W. Norton & Company, Inc.
500 Fifth Avenue, New York, N.Y. 10110
W. W. Norton & Company Ltd.
37 Great Russell Street, London WC1B 3NU

    2 3 4 5 6 7 8 9 0

To the beloved mentally ill of all families

THE SCHIZOPHRENIC BLUES

Walking with sadness in my shoes, leaving footprints
of schizophrenic blues
As I journey feeling blue, searching for happiness
long overdue—
Feelings of anguish and aching defeat trot along
beneath my feet
And seeing my child with pale vacant eyes gives
steps to not caring if I live or die—
So I'll kick up my heels, put a dance in my shoes
and try to chase away the schizophrenic blues.

LILLIAN M. PELLEGRINI

Contents

Foreword by Henry Grunebaum, M.D.   ix

Introduction by Carol Smith, M.S.W.   xv

Preface by Nona Dearth, for the Collective   xix

1. From Initial Shock to Acceptance   1
2. From the Hospital to Home and Back Again   17
3. How Brothers and Sisters See It   32
4. The Rights and Wrongs of Patients' Rights   56
5. Keeping a Life of One's Own   66
6. Dealing With Professionals   78
7. Beyond Talk Therapy and Pills   87
8. Smiling Through the Tears   102
9. Dreaming for the Future   114
10. How Can We Change Things Now?   129
11. Reaching Out Through Networking   140

Afterword   153

Notes   155

Affiliates of the National Alliance for the
Mentally Ill   157

Foreword

Or what man is there of you, whom if his son asks for bread, will he give him a stone?
—MATTHEW 7:9.

If you have a son or daughter, a husband or wife, a brother or sister, or someone else you love who has schizophrenia or another chronic mental illness, here is the place to learn about how to live with them, their illness, yourself, and the other people in your life. This book is written by the experts, the families of the mentally ill, the only people who know what life in that tragic situation is like because they have lived it themselves. If you are a professional, there is much you can learn, as I did, from the families of our patients if you are willing to listen to them unencumbered by theoretical preconceptions.

In this regard, it is, perhaps, useful to say something about how I became involved with these parents and, thus, with this book, for my journey is an example of the journey of American psychiatry. I was trained in the era when it was believed that mothers caused childhood autism and began doing family therapy when families were believed to cause schizophrenia. In 1976 I came to Westboro State Hospital at the invitation of then superintendent Lawrence Schiff, Ph.D., a very caring man, to teach the staff how to work more effectively with the families they met there. Gradually, I began doing demonstration interviews with patients and their families and found a home on the Framingham-Natick unit with the support of the area director, Sanford Autor, Ph.D.

As the years went by and I continued to teach and consult, I found myself increasingly interviewing families whom I had first encountered some years earlier. Then my focus had been, consistent with my training and my own research, "How has this family contributed to the illness of this child?" Over the years, however, as I began to see the same families struggling with the pain of repeated hospitalizations, my point of view changed. The precipitants of schizophrenia seemed less relevant than the family's efforts to help the patient and to live their own lives. Often the families asked me, "What will happen after we are dead?" and at other times they seemed to behave as though either this would never happen or the patient would miraculously get well. Slowly the ethical and existential nature of the predicament became clearer. I began to wonder, "What is the illness of this child doing to this family, and how can we help them both cope better?" Perhaps some of the change was due to the emergence of my own children into adolescence and my increasing awareness, probably defensive, that influences work both ways. Perhaps some was due to the new research which made it increasingly evident that while the parents' role in the genesis of schizophrenia was unproven, their ways of dealing with their adult child had a major impact on the outcome.[1]

Around 1979, Carol Smith, M.S.W., the social worker in charge of aftercare, became actively involved in developing support programs for parents in our catchment area, with advice from James Beck, M.D., a member of the staff of the Cambridge Hospital and a researcher on schizophrenia. She and I were regularly discussing the issues presented by the various families who were participating in the aftercare program, many of whom I knew from my own contacts. From this matrix, the idea arose that these parents could be enabled to write a book growing out of their experiences which would be of value to other parents, and to professionals. And over the years that the parents group has met, the project has become their project and the book is their book. We have changed our views of each other as we moved from being psychiatrists, social workers, and clients to being colleagues. Our mutual affection and respect have similarly grown.

The journey I traveled has been traveled by American psychiatry as well. The hopeless prognosis for mental illness prior to the fifties, which had led to the warehousing of patients in the state mental hospitals, gave way to the optimism of the sixties and the burgeoning of the community mental health movement. It was thought that with the various psychotherapies and pharmacotherapy almost all patients could be helped to live satisfactory lives in the community. A vast program of discharging patients to their communities and homes was begun long before adequate services for them were available. And it fell to the parents of these individuals to fill the gap between the hospital on the one hand, eager to discharge patients for clinical and economic reasons and mandated to do so because of concern with the civil rights of patients, and the community on the other hand, where services for aftercare, rehabilitation, and living were frequently unavailable and even refused by the patient.

At the present time most chronic psychotic patients will spend the major portion of their lives in the community. There they will have to manage for themselves with the aid and support of mental health professionals, community resources, and their families. However, community living increases the likelihood that the patient will suffer illness or accident because of defects in judgment, impaired sense of reality, and poor choice of companions. Clearly the risk of suicide is greater.

Today we nonetheless believe that patients may fare better in the long run if they learn to make it on their own—a task for which they lack many basic skills. At times of stress patients often turn to community resources and mental health professionals, but in the end they are most likely to turn to their families who are their court of last appeal. Families know that ultimately patients are better off learning to make it on their own. After all, patients will generally outlive their parents. But when will they be left to survive alone, and how do the parents insist that they make it on their own? Families soon learn that patients' appeals are sometimes manipulations but are often desperate cries for help. On what appeal and at what time do they finally say "No"? Families also know that while community living involves a considerable and unknown degree of risk to the patient, life in the hospital is a kind of death, a slow one. On the other hand, in the hospital patients will be fed, have a roof over their heads, be clothed, and to a great extent be protected from their impulses; further, by and large, the caretakers they encounter will be well intentioned. Still, this alternative is being phased out for many patients.

Clearly, a collaboration between mental health professionals and the families of the patients is both necessary and appropriate. Furthermore, research[2] has demonstrated that family-centered psychoeducational approaches are effective in reducing relapse rates. But not only is such collaboration necessary, appropriate, and effective, it is also an ethical necessity, for families labor under the major burden, and they also are human with their own claims for a decent life. A family does not work a five-day week nor an eight-hour day. In addition, it is the families who are faced with the most difficult questions.

John Talbott, M.D., past President of the American Psychiatric Association, recently echoed a growing professional understanding of the families' burden:

> It is impossible to decide whether or not to continue medication to someone previously unmanageable who is developing early signs of side effects; to choose between a fine long-term facility and a working farm; to know whether a trip to a long-lost relative in California represents escape or an attempt at reintegration into the family; or to advise on whether to seek placement for a patient in a nursing home because his parents, who are visibly and rapidly aging, can no longer care for him at home. But these are questions that families engage in every day and sharing in the struggle sometimes makes them more bearable.[3]

In the last analysis the answers to these questions are not based on clinical expertise; they are based on moral judgments. What does one owe oneself as a parent and what does one owe one's mentally ill child? What does one give of one's always limited resources to the child who needs the most and what to the child with the better chances for a productive life? What does one owe one's marriage and what does one owe one's own aging parents? The answers to these questions are not in the textbooks of psychiatry. The answers to these questions are part of the lives of the parents of the mentally ill and, thus, part of this book.

Henry Grunebaum, M.D.
Cambridge, MA
January, 1986

Introduction

The Follow-up Team in Framingham, Massachusetts is an aftercare service for Westboro State Hospital with the responsibility to case-manage patients leaving the hospital and moving to the community.

During my early training as a social worker, Henry Grunebaum, M.D., taught me that it was important to work with the whole family, and this we are doing. In 1978, James Beck, M.D., also teaching at the Westboro State Hospital, asked if anyone would be interested in starting a psychoeducational group for families of the mentally ill. I was.

In September 1979, with Jim Beck's supervision, along with Judith Scott and Katherine Greer, we established our first psychoeducational series held in the community for families of the mentally ill. The long-range plan was to enable families leaving the first group to start their own local self-help group. It is now a reality. With the leadership of the late Harold Cohen, M.D., the families established the Alliance for the Mentally Ill (AMI) of Middlesex County, Inc. They then supported and advised other groups that were organized, and they were active in establishing a statewide alliance. In turn both the local and state alliances have joined forces with the National Alliance for the Mentally Ill.

Families of the mentally ill in the South Middlesex area of Massachusetts, like families everywhere, knew very little about what professionals were writing about them, and what they read they didn't like. We asked the families who had come to the parents' education groups at our agency to start writing about mental illness from their perspective. Initially this idea of their writing about their experiences was not a concept they understood. But they have gradually come to see that they have a unique and valuable point of view. They have changed and so have we professionals. The changes are exciting.

In early 1982 six parents, Dr. Grunebaum, Blair Gelbond, aftercare therapist/case manager, and myself founded the writers group that developed this book. Being part of this group has been both a joyous and painful experience. Much laughter and much pain have been shared. The first few months the writers needed to come to trust one another. The material written often did not capture the feeling and experience of what the family members had shared in the group. But as time went on, as the family members and professionals became more honest with one another, the families' material began to reflect the true experience of what it is like to live with a family member who is ill before any diagnosis has been made, what it is like to take a loved one to a hospital for the first time, and what frustrations and fears are felt when the family needs to trust but often does not trust the professional.

The families have shared how they withdrew from family and friends while they were experiencing this terrible pain of mental illness, and finally how they learned to use and establish a network of support groups, which eventually involved them as advocates, speakers, teachers, and writers. With more than 100 families in the local group, more than 2500 members in the state group, and more than 50,000 in the national group, families' power is beginning to be felt. These families are effecting changes in services, research, and treatment.

We, the families and the professionals, are doing a better job teaching one another about mental illness. The professionals share relevant research material with the families, material that deals with setting limits with their ill member, effecting separations, resuming activities as couples, grieving about the illness, and in general dealing with good parenting for mentally ill family members. The families in return teach us what it is like to live with mental illness in the family. We, the professionals, are more conscious of the patients and what their needs are. For instance, we have learned what it is like for them not to be able to get services they need in hospitals or community programs, or most of all what it is like not to be heard by the professionals. The families have experienced more directly than anyone what the family members need. With this mutual learning from one another, our goal is for families and professionals to teach other professionals and families the benefits of using an educational model where both groups learn from one another. We have taught this philosophy at hospital rounds, colleges, seminars, agencies, and other family groups.

There is much more to do but a start has been made. Join them as families. Join them as professionals.

Carol Smith, M.S.W.
Framingham, MA
January, 1986

Preface

Writing this book has been a labor of love and of pain, born of necessity. If it helps lighten the burden of one family with a seriously mentally ill member—a burden of guilt, bewilderment, fear and frustration—then the three years we have worked to write it will have been well spent.

All of us involved with this book know the agony of suddenly finding ourselves in the unreal world of chronic mental illness without knowing where to turn for help and understanding. Some of us struggled alone for five to ten years. We know parents who have spent the better part of their lives carrying this terrible burden alone. The tragedy, when chronic mental illness strikes a child, is more than any family should have to cope with without support.

This book has been written to help families cope, to let them know what they will be facing, to ease the burden, and to educate the public so that families won't have to battle the devastating stigma of mental illness at the same time that they are trying to cope with the illness itself in their sons and daughters.

Every chapter but one in this book has been written totally by family members who have a chronically mentally ill relative. The only exception is the chapter on siblings' reactions. In that chapter, the unifying text has been written by Blair Gelbond, a therapist trained in family therapy and psychosynthesis who, with Carol Smith, began a mutual learning group of siblings and professionals. The personal stories, of course, are by the brothers and sisters themselves.

We gratefully thank all the siblings who contributed to this book as well as the families not in the Collective who gave us their stories.

We also acknowledge our deep appreciation to Priscilla Mercurio for helping to write the unifying texts, to Joan Holt for her typing endurance, to Kathy Norman for her suggestions, to Carolyn Mercer-McFadden for her editorial advice, to Ralph Crawshaw, M.D., of Portland, OR, for his critique, to Attorneys Elizabeth Kunz and Anthony G. Pellegrini for their legal advice, to Michael J. DeCesare, CPA, for his business advice, to The Boston Women's Health Book Collective, authors of *Our Bodies, Ourselves,* for general information on how they wrote collectively, and to Henry Grunebaum and Carol Smith for planting the seed and nourishing it with their constant encouragement.

Nona Dearth, Chairman
Families of the Mentally
Ill Collective

FAMILIES
HELPING
FAMILIES

Living With Schizophrenia

Chapter 1

From Initial Shock to Acceptance

There is no end to the suffering when a son or a daughter has chronic mental illness but the suffering becomes more bearable when it is shared, when families know what the real problems are and what the answers might be. Until a level of hope is reached, each parent travels a long road of heartbreak and frustration. Finally, there may be some hope. The purpose of this book is to give that hope.

According to the National Alliance for the Mentally Ill, severe mental illness devastates the lives of close to three million Americans and affects close to 15 million family members. Mental illness is the number one reason for hospital admissions in this country, and one-fourth of the mentally ill admitted to hospitals are diagnosed as having schizophrenia. That is more than the number of patients with cancer, heart disease, diabetes and debilitating arthritis combined. And yet, in spite of these overwhelming and frightening statistics, funding for research and for the care of the mentally ill has always been less than for other diseases. These facts add to the anguish of parents.

There is no point in offering false encouragement. There is no magical swift cure for long-term mental illness. There is not even agreement on its causes and, in fact, there are probably many causes: genetic, biochemical, trauma. It is generally accepted now that the cause of severe schizophrenia is genetic and / or biological, a fact that, unfortunately, has been too often ignored by "couch-prone" psychiatrists. There is also a schizophrenia brought on by extreme trauma. Research may change the whys and wherefores at any time.

There is also little agreement on treatment and, no doubt, a variety of treatments may be valid for a variety of individuals. But of one thing we can be certain—the mental and emotional pain suffered by the family as well as the patient is horrendous. There are no soft words to describe it.

Even before you know what it's called, it's like a living hell.

My son Danny sits next to me and says, "Mom! Do you know that I'm Jesus? I found out that I'm really Jesus!"

My face freezes into a crooked smile. I search his face for an answer and see by his look and manner that he is sincere in an unhealthy way. My whole being seems to leave my chair, and I become suspended in air for what seems to be an eternity. Tumbling down, I spin like a top with astounding speed, then go crashing into the wall with such great force that I bounce back into my chair. My numb, aching body now waits, hoping and praying that the earth will open up and swallow me.

I was told that as long as it took Danny to get sick, that's how long it would take for him to get better. My mind would race. One year? Two? Five? When did it actually begin? But seeing my son with vacant eyes, bizarre behavior, unnatural movements, pacing back and forth, it became hard for me to believe this theory. I knew his illness was too serious, and it was here to stay. Was it an inner feeling, my common sense or something only a mother knows?

Day by day as Danny's condition worsened, his emptiness was reflected in me. I began to lose hope and a hold on life. My own eyes became vacant as I lost sight of any beauty around me. I was becoming more and more like a robot, doing only what had to be done. The excruciating pain penetrated my entire being.

At one point, when I would sit for hours praying, I pondered the story of when Jesus was presented to the Lord, and Simeon foretold how the sword that would pierce Jesus would also pierce the soul of Mary. I had always understood it but now I identified with her pain, and my heart went out to Mary.

It is often said that out of bad comes good. I hope some good will come out of my son's suffering, for his sake and for the sake of all the mentally ill and their families. Because after it's called schizophrenia so you know what it is, it's still like a living hell.

Chronic mental illness—which is most often severe schizophrenia—is so difficult to cope with because the patient's actions and reactions are irrational to the observer but completely logical to the schizophrenic. Parents see a stranger, an off-the-wall son or daughter who refuses to shape up. The sick child inhabits a different world and that world, consciously or unconsciously, terrifies the parents. They don't know how to handle it; they don't want to accept it. Generally, children and parents back away from each other. There is no common meeting ground. Even love cannot bridge the gap.

Eccentric. Willful. Disobedient. Psychoneurotic. Playing games. Deliberately hurtful. Childish.

These were some of the words I used to describe Lora when her illness first became apparent. For me, it was an illness that had no name. I knew only that my daughter was not behaving normally, that, in fact, her actions were outrageous.

I became angry at her. She is an intelligent person, and suddenly she was acting without intelligence. She was a very talented actress, dancer, and choreographer, and she was letting her career go down the drain as she became more and more enmeshed with pacts made in heaven, as she talked directly to God and Jesus and the archangels, as she made pacts with Lucifer in order to save the world. It was insane.

But even as I thought her actions were insane, I didn't imagine that my daughter could *be* insane. Not *my* daughter. It was impossible. I was often angry at her. Why couldn't she behave? Why was she being so impossible? I was hurt to the point of numbness when she said she didn't want to talk to me, didn't want to see me, when she told me she hated me. At other times I was frustrated and distraught. And always guilt-stricken. What had I done wrong? No mother is perfect but I must have been worse than most for my daughter to act as she did.

The fact that Lora was in New York and I was in Boston when her first breaks came didn't help matters. Telephone conversations can be frustrating. It is easy to bang down the phone in fury—which we both did on occasion. It was not much better when I would take a day off from work, ride to New York on the bus, visit her at one or another of the three hospitals she entered—the visits always frustrating—and return home the same day on the bus, exhausted. At times I wished I was in the hospital with her, being taken care of.

Well-meaning friends told me there was nothing I could do to help her, that it was not my fault that she acted as she did, that she would be better only when she wanted to be better. Everybody knew, they would say, that neurotics, like alcoholics, could be helped only when they wanted to be. Nobody used the word *psychotic* when they were being sympathetic about my problems. Psychotic meant crazy and nobody wanted to imply *that*. I myself refused to face that. The stigma, the shame, the possibility of forever . . . it was impossible to face that.

Even when she came home and was hospitalized locally and I was told that the diagnosis was schizophrenia—a *classic* case of schizophrenia, I was told—even then I didn't let it register as an actual thing that had a stranglehold on my daughter. I was sure there had to be an answer and a cure if only I looked long enough. I could not accept the fact of real insanity. My pride and my guilt worked against me so that I couldn't admit the simple truth of a psychosis.

But as I looked for cures and answers, I also learned more about schizophrenia, and I could no longer ignore the facts. Then, though my guilt feelings lessened, the heartbreak grew. There was so little that could be done. If schizophrenia is genetic and / or biochemical—which I firmly believe—then Lora could not be blamed for her actions and her thoughts, could not be held totally accountable for what she did. Her thoughts and her actions grew out of a real physical disability, and until a cure was found she would remain schizophrenic. Under present circumstances she might be stabilized but not cured.

It was hard for me to accept that, even though it did reduce my feelings of guilt. It is still a heartbreaking fact to accept.

Almost without exception, coping with the onslaught of chronic mental illness is more than parents can face. They try to ignore it. They try to rationalize it. They become angry, bewildered, resentful, truly stricken with fear and guilt. Since the parents are unaware that schizophrenia is slowly taking over the mind of their child, the illness shatters their lives almost as much as it does the child's when it becomes apparent. Usually, there are few overt signs of what is coming.

Undoubtedly if Thomas had not developed this tragic illness, the behavior of his early years would not be that unusual. It would remain in the background and be considered as a phase in his development, if considered at all. However, as I look back I now realize that his behavior in his early years was a prelude to the unfortunate affliction. I can recall so many areas where he was difficult.

Even as a baby, when our son resented whatever wasn't to his liking, he would scream and cry almost endlessly. In one instance I recall, we took him to the pediatrician, when he was ten months old, to be checked. He cried and carried on so that the doctor suggested that unless something urgent came up, he wouldn't need regular checkups since he really seemed to be all right. Any change in his feeding routine would be a major ordeal.

As a young boy, Thomas would insist on doing things which he knew perfectly well were the wrong things to do, and yet he felt compelled to do them. After such an episode, he would tell me he was sorry and that he really loved me.

He felt the need to attract attention in any way possible. In groups that he belonged to he would appear late at an appointed meeting and in that way attract attention to himself and disrupt the meeting. After a while, he was excluded from groups, and the feeling of rejection added to his aggression.

Whenever Thomas attended any kind of function or movie, on returning home he would be restless and unhappy instead of being satisfied. On many occasions, once he reached his destination he would want to go on to something else. Contentment was not one of his strong areas.

As our son is intelligent and, in fact, has a bachelor's degree and credits toward his master's, one might expect that he would have enjoyed reading for the pleasure of it. However, I don't remember that he would read a book unless he had to give a report, and then he did it hurriedly. His repetitive characteristic showed up early when he would play the same record over and over again on his record player.

Towards his last two years in high school, Thomas started to be suspicious of people. He really surprised me when he refused an invitation to a party given by some of his peers whom he had known for a number of years. He actually said he was afraid and did not attend. Before that he did like parties. Without realizing it at the time, it was a definite change in his personality. It was the beginning of the rough road with so many detours that our son's life was to embark upon.

The illness strikes at a most vulnerable time, usually from the middle teens to the late twenties, when young people are on the threshold of their future. It strikes at every economic and social level. There are patients who have earned their doctorates, others who were in the arts, some who were in banking and business, and many who had not yet had time to find themselves.

No matter how many early signs there are that assume significance once the illness becomes acute, the first severe break comes as a shock to the parents.

It seemed to have started quite abruptly. Jean, our 19-year-old daughter, seemed to have everything going for her. She had many friends and was attending college. Then all that changed one day. She was very upset and announced she was dropping out of college.

But looking back, the changes that took place in her personality were very noticeable. She had crying spells on and off for no apparent reason and began to affect bizarre behavior patterns such as having her hair cut extremely short, gazing out of windows, seeing imaginary black cars in the driveway and hearing voices threatening to kill her. She was scared to death—and so was the rest of the family. We felt so helpless!

There were also incidents of outbursts from her outside the house. During a family vacation, on our way to church, she started to scream and kick us, right out of the blue. She looked at us like strangers, with fear in her eyes. Another incident found her calling us incoherently from her new job with the notion that some of her fellow workers were going to beat her up. Jean disappeared for several hours, and when we finally located her, she was screaming uncontrollably.

In light of her highly unusual behavior, we determined that Jean may have suffered a nervous breakdown. We consulted our family physician, and he advised us to send our daughter to a prominent local psychiatrist.

Sadly, Jean was diagnosed as having schizophrenia.

Even when there are telltale signs of trouble brewing, parents don't recognize them for what they are. And there is no reason why they should. Parents who have lived through the teenage years of their children—even when they grow up to be so-called normal adults—learn to ignore or accept the moody, changing, annoying, ludicrous shifts of habits and interests.

When I look back now, I realize there were warning signs but, like most parents, I regarded them as "stages" that Lora would outgrow. Early shyness and excessive moodiness that I equated with her delightful pixie-like appearance. An inability to sit still in school that started in the first grade and lasted through high school. Swings in mood from almost hysterical enthusiasm and extraordinary bursts of concentration to depression, negative attitudes and a seeming inability to concentrate on anything for more than a brief period. But teenagers, I thought, are a mysterious, ever-changing breed of people so I took Lora's troubling mood changes as part of a natural growing up process.

It was during the summer when she was 17 that overt signs of future trouble surfaced. For many years we have spent summer vacations in Provincetown where a person's individuality is respected and nobody questions what you do or how you live. Dress is casual. But suddenly Lora was dressing like a man—baggy pants, oversized shirt, and a cloth cap with her beautiful long black hair messily piled up underneath it. She looked like a caricature of herself. She was questioning her sexuality. She had three older brothers she thought were superior to herself, smarter and more talented. Did she want to be one of the brothers?

Even when professional advice is sought in the early stages of this terrible illness, help is not necessarily forthcoming. Doctors, too, do not know, or recognize, the first signs of schizophrenia—probably because the signs are so variable. It isn't until a young person has a personality break or builds up a history of unusual behavior that the mental illness becomes apparent.

It started with "It isn't easy to raise a teenager." It became "This must be hell."

David, who had always been a life-loving, ambitious, cooperative and sociable lad blessed with good health and good looks, became indecisive and sometimes stubborn and excessive. There is no scientific evidence that his present condition can be traced back to an earlier year when he was leaving childhood, grade school, and parental care—but that was the year when my husband and I found David on the floor one pre-dawn morning for the first time, recovering from what we later learned was a seizure. We dismissed it as an overreaction to a bad dream.

Not until this experience had repeated itself did we feel it necessary to seek the advice of a neurologist. He optimistically told us, "This fine young man is reacting to fatigue and will probably not have a recurrence. Treat him as you would normally but I would suggest that he not swim alone or do any mountain climbing." Subsequent seizures led to subsequent doctors as we moved in the interim, and David went off to prep school. No medications were prescribed. Rather, it seems to me now that more attention was given to us, his mother and father, to alleviate our concern and anxiety.

It was probably two or three years from the onset that

the first real distress signal was sounded. David had graduated from prep school and had dropped out of college after the first month. As a last resort, we sought a psychiatrist. I say "as a last resort" because, although it is hard to believe today, ten years ago asking for help from the psychiatric world was a real admission of failure. Our doctor described David's situation as "like walking on eggs," in anticipation of his next seizure. But our son was not in a mind to ask for help. Still, no medication was prescribed for his condition, which perhaps would have tempered the strain and apprehension he was under even though his seizures had been diagnosed as temporary, which indeed proved to be true.

My husband and I continued to have faith that David would flourish and mature. Hadn't the doctor's prognosis been positive? Hadn't my father assured me that everything would work out? There was no history of epilepsy in our families. Not to worry. Hadn't I been assured throughout my childhood and as an adult that God would answer our prayers for healing? And so we continued to act on the premise that there was really no need for concern. After all, the seizures were not debilitating and happened rarely. And if we didn't mention it to anyone, no one would know, and David wouldn't have to suffer the prejudice and discrimination that epileptics suffer. It would go away. And it was true. The seizures did go away.

But something was wrong, and our son still "was walking on eggs." When the seizures stopped, the bizarre behavior began. David's actions were excessive in every area. If he cleaned his room, it was a tornado at work. If he took a walk, his neck craned, searching the tree tops. He worked beside his brothers with multiracial field hands in a nursery and would stop and sing in a loud voice at will and often. He, who once adored one brother and cared for the younger with endearment, now was indifferent and often abrasive toward them, yet leaped to defend a stranger in an altercation, to his own disadvantage. It happened when working in the fields that the blacks and hispanics would abuse and

insult each other. David would rally to the side of the under-
dog, escalating the altercation and isolating himself—to find
his own job threatened.

I continue to pray for our son's healing, and my faith
in God grows as I continue to believe in the God beyond the
God that says "No." His care and support, comfort and light
have brought to me a new and richer appreciation for life
and for love, of my husband and children, my friends and
country. I have a new love of self. I know that God's answer
to my prayer is not always "Yes," at least in my timing, but
to my life His answer *is* "Yes."

The first time parents deal with a psychiatric hospital,
private or state-operated, it is usually a traumatic experience. Seeing the door shut on a closed ward causes a stab
of pain that is never forgotten. Too few hospitals for the
mentally ill are helpful; too many are totally ineffective.
But sometimes there are dedicated, caring staff members
who can make a difference.

Jim's first admission to a psychiatric hospital was the ulti-
mate disaster. This was my fatherly reaction at the time. Now
I am thankful for the event and wish that it might have come
about several years earlier.

My son was displaying sufficient unusual behavior in
second grade to cause him to be referred to the school psychologist. I went to a series of interviews with this lady, and
we talked at length about his difficulties with school work
and his troubled relationships with other children. I was never
convinced there was very much wrong and, in fact, quite
resented the inference that there was. My judgment seemed
borne out by the temporary cessation of the troubles.

When Jim was nine, our move to another neighbor-
hood required an adjustment to an initially hostile and highly
competitive group of children. He seemed to weather these
circumstances well, having a good school record, including

varsity football through junior year in high school. Jim was then once more uprooted by a family move. His senior year in another town and another school was difficult, with new relationships not readily established. He did manage to be accepted by one of the colleges of his choice and went away there with some outward enthusiasm.

Within six weeks I was summoned by school authorities because Jim was "depressed," and there had been talk of suicide. I found him in a state of bewilderment and panic, from which he could be drawn by assurance that he might come home. I took him home, and he went to a psychiatrist for a year. The problem was supposed to be a "mood disturbance," with eventual relief thought most likely. Jim was encouraged to seek work and defer academic activity for a year or two.

He steadily declined into a state of extraordinary indolence, almost constantly on his bed, either sleeping or smoking or listening to rock music at top volume. At first, he would take a job but these never lasted more than a few weeks. He would always get terminated for entirely inadequate performance. Jim's younger brother moved upstairs from a large room and bath they had shared, unable to stand his slothful habits and unpleasant talk. Jim would invade his sister's room, creating loud scenes and occasionally striking her. They had formerly been especially close. His mother became unable to tolerate his ways, or his presence in the house, and when she would tell him so, he would strike her.

For many months I resisted the advice of a psychiatrist that I get Jim out of the house. Then, about two years from the beginning of the trouble, I put him out, with assistance from the community mental health service in finding housing and setting up a program for him. There followed a dreadful series of encounters when he broke in, battered down doors, and otherwise terrorized the household. On those occasions the police would be called, and they would come and make him go back where he belonged.

Finally he was taken to a hospital emergency ward when

he stated he had taken an overdose of his medication. This resulted in his first admission to a psychiatric hospital. It was decided that he was schizophrenic. There followed five years of intermittent hospital stays and disastrous attempts at community placement, while his unreasonable fears became increasingly bizarre. Visions and voices beset him; he would go off his medication and strange paralyses occurred. Then Jim slowly and sporadically began to do better.

It was a long and very rocky course, but I would now think of the first admission as the beginning of the correct recognition of the problem and the proper handling of it. I would recommend to those confronted with this grim necessity to look upon it with some optimism.

The old buildings of long established state institutions which are still in use in many parts of the country can be frightening and forbidding. Often prison-like in construction, they add to the terror and gloom experienced by parents approaching them for the first time, and that feeling can continue for a long time. It is unbearable to them to think that those buildings are now home to their children. Acceptance comes slowly; it can come in many ways.

I remember I feared that one day my son David might be confined in a mental hospital. If I entered the building myself, would I have difficulty getting out? Frequently I drove past the state institution in the next town and was chilled by the austerity of the block-like buildings and dark windows.

Knowing ignorance is the basis of much fear, I stopped one day outside the administration building. I was nervous and trembling a little. I kept my left glove on to cover my wedding ring and sought the volunteer office. I was directed to the second floor by an attendant who answered my question by assuring me that I'd have no trouble leaving. "It's easier to get out than it is to get in," he said. And truly that was the case. Indeed, the director was pleased to add my name to her list of volunteers. A weekly visit to the hospital took very little time from my usual routine.

Soon the institution took on a new image. It was people now, not just brick and mortar and terror. It was a young girl who admired my jewelry and occasionally ended up with the inexpensive pin on her dress. It was a young boy asking for his cigarettes and an old lady who winced if you shook her arthritic hand too hard. Sadness yes, but no longer fear for myself when I visited the hospital.

Sometimes it seems to a parent that he or she will never be able to approach the hospital without feeling a wrenching heartache, a terrible nightmarish feeling in the pit of the stomach, at the sight of those buildings. But the human spirit is indeed indomitable, and strength is found when it is needed.

How do you muster courage when you're alone, after you've driven some hours to visit your son who's been retained in an out-of-state hospital? Sometimes just entering the building drains your strength. Often it's a small thing that carries one through. I remember as I approached one hospital building I said to myself, "Breathe deeply. Breathe in the good, exhale the bad, breathe in the good, exhale the bad, breathe in the good." Then I was on the second floor, and there was a call for David, and he was all that mattered.

"Hi, Mom. Are you okay?"

Yes, I was.

Reading the stories of parents who have gone through the traumatic experience of learning that a child has chronic mental illness, listening to them at meetings of support groups, it becomes clear that there are no definitive answers as to why one sibling is stricken with mental illness and another is not, no diagnosis that positively defines the illness, no particular way to handle the parental trauma. Each case, each person, is unique. Each parent finds his or her own staff of faith.

Diagnosis and treatment are so varied that parents new to the weird world of chronic mental illness become thoroughly confused and frustrated as they try to find help for the afflicted child. Then they finally realize that the great majority of doctors and other professionals don't have any answers, that they, too, are groping in an unknown world. After ten years of watching his or her child go through the heart-wrenching cycles of schizophrenia, almost any parent knows as much, if not more, about effective care of the disease as any psychiatrist. But living through the dreadful period of not knowing or understanding what is happening and then reaching a modicum of acceptance can result, finally, in some hope.

When I came out of the closet to work openly for improvement in the lives of the mentally ill through the Alliance for the Mentally Ill, I found there were hundreds of other parents who had suffered the same guilt and frustrations I had. And still do.

But now, working and sharing with others has opened new doors, has opened my eyes to new possibilities. There is exciting research in the field of nutrition, revealing the importance of a proper diet and supplemental vitamins and minerals. Research is showing the importance of removing stress from the life of a schizophrenic. A pleasant environment is now known to be helpful. Regular exercise and athletic activities have been proven beneficial. New medication with fewer side effects is coming out of the laboratories.

Parents of the chronically mentally ill are fighting openly and passionately for more research, for better living conditions, for public understanding and compassion. They are going into the community to fight the stigma of mental illness. They are going to state legislators for better laws and more funding. They are going to the federal level for more research.

There is, finally, a glimmer of progress just beyond the horizon.

Chapter 2

From the Hospital to Home and Back Again

The first discharge from the hospital for the chronically mentally ill patient is seldom an optimistic landmark on the road to recovery. In most illnesses, discharge means progress has been made. Not so with chronic schizophrenia. Instead, it usually means that under medication a level of ability to cope, to some extent, has been reached—with the warning that there may be a swing back to an inability to cope, which happens more often than not. That is the bitter truth under present methods of treatment in the great majority of hospitals and clinics. The cycle seems to be constant and seemingly hopeless for the patient and for the family.

Lora's first hospitalizations were in New York, and since I lived and worked in Boston, I had little understanding of what was happening. Each time she was discharged, I was pleased that she was better. When she was soon readmitted, I was puzzled and emotionally devastated. This cycle of events happened four times in New York. I felt like a pingpong ball being emotionally battered, back and forth, none of it making any sense.

Eventually Lora called me and asked if she could come home to rest and pull herself together. In the midst of her schizophrenia she can have lucid, logical periods. At first her visit home was very pleasant. It was nice to have her there, to talk to her, to have the table set for dinner when I came home from work. But then the cycle started to swing. She would stay up most of the night, playing records, smoking, talking to her spirits. There would be sudden bursts of hysterical laughter. Her actions and reactions became more and more erratic. Finally, I came home from work one night and found the table set for four people. She explained that God and the psychiatrist she had adored were coming to dinner.

Her intensity, her disjointed conversation, her flash of anger when I protested—they all frightened me. I called my son who lived closest to me—in Amherst, an hour-and-a-half drive—and asked him to make the trip so we could take Lora to the hospital. I didn't dare drive her to the hospital alone. I also needed family support. He came immediately, and we took her to the Framingham Union Hospital emergency room where, after several hours of waiting, Lora was admitted to the psychiatric ward. That was the start of her hospitalization in Massachusetts. She has never gone back to New York.

For more than a year, Lora was in and out of Framingham Union. A short-term facility as pleasant as a country club, the psychiatric unit there became her security blanket, a place she could run to whenever life became more than she could cope with. The staff recognized the pattern and finally sent her to Westboro State Hospital, hoping the shock of being there would set her on the path to sanity. How could so many well-meaning professional people know so little about the care and handling of acute schizophrenia? Instead of being shocked into sanity, Lora embraced ward insanity, set about to save the world from her new base and set herself up as the nun of the hospital. Consciously or unconsciously, her sense of the dramatic never left her.

Lora has always been a voluntary patient—I do not have the heart to legally commit her—so on several occasions she has signed herself out. Each occasion has ended in catastrophe, and she has gone back to the state hospital. Once when she rented an apartment, she went into the foyer at three o'clock in the morning and rang the bell to every apartment to tell the residents she was saving the world. She was sent back to Westboro. It was after that episode, when I saw her on the ward, that she said she didn't ever want to go back into the world because people were too cruel. But she has been back several times, each time rebounding from each disaster—just long enough to create another catastrophe from which to recover.

Parents are beset by conflicting emotions after the first hospital discharge of a son or daughter. They feel hope and fear, guilt and confusion, all intertwining, not knowing where one begins and one ends.

In hope, you feel that the worst may be over, and the ill member will slowly progress. In fear, you remember how severely ill he or she was and wonder if it will start again and if it does, how you will cope and how you can suppress your fear. In guilt, you wonder where you went wrong and if you should have done things differently.

Then comes confusion. Are you able to have your son or daughter live with you? Can you handle it? Other people live with their handicapped children. Why can't you? Are you selfish, abnormal or weak? Decisions become cloudy at this time and must be made slowly in order to sort everything out in its proper place.

Parents of long-term schizophrenics soon learn to condition themselves to the fact that their sons and daughters will need to be institutionalized repeatedly. Accepting that fact makes each trip back to the hospital more or less expected and, eventually, less painful. Even so, hope never really dies, and it is probably this small reserve of faith in eventual improvement that makes it possible for parents to survive, to visit and encourage their mentally ill children with expressions of love and to forge a bond of trust between them. This is, in fact, an important therapy for the patient.

On his first discharge from the hospital, it seemed that Thomas' problems were under control. A program of outpatient therapy and medication was recommended while he was living at home. However, it didn't go all that smoothly. Living at home, he was soon back to spending much time in bed, reluctant to adhere to a schedule.

He did get to a few sessions at the hospital which involved therapy and some workshops. Attending these sessions was always difficult for him because his desire to resume school was so great. It was finally decided that school would be the best therapy for Thomas, with some follow-up care included. This became a very happy time for him. Arrangements were being made for his return to his college studies. He was buying books and arranging for dormitory living. It really seemed that he would take up where he had left off.

Unfortunately, it didn't work that way. When Thomas shared living quarters with another student, the arrangement didn't last very long, and that in itself would set up disappointments and a feeling of rejection. Thomas would spend much of the time in the dormitory and not attend classes. His room would become more and more untidy. Then, after some time of inactivity, his father would move his belongings out of the dormitory and bring him home. After he was home for some time and really unable to function, we would have to resort to hospitalization for Thomas once again, much to our sorrow.

The realization that our son's condition has required repeated hospitalization has been a most painful one. But we are grateful that there are facilities to care for Thomas when coping becomes impossible for him.

It often seems to parents that patients are discharged even though they don't meet the criteria for discharge. They still are unable to take care of themselves or may be a danger to themselves or others.

Early discharge and lack of follow-up create conditions that make psychotic cycles recur rapidly. Cycles may be brought on by stress or lack of medication and proper diet. These cycles are different for each individual. Some may begin to sleep all day, neither eating nor bathing. Many run to various parts of the country. Others constantly pace back and forth to the point of completely wearing themselves out. Others may have continuous, non-sensible verbalization or hysterical laughter.

Doctors very seldom tell families about these cycles, even when asked. Their reply at times is, "There is no way of knowing." But, in fact, almost every schizophrenic lives in cycles, and it is important for relatives to ask about them, insisting on answers, because the cycles will become a way of life.

Danny had received an associate degree in architectural engineering, and the future looked bright. A year later he suffered his first mental breakdown. At that time he was living at his grandmother's house. He was admitted to a private hospital for one week, and since we were in a state of shock and unable to comprehend the severity of his illness, we refused the advice of the psychiatrist to send him to a psychiatric hospital. Too many negative feelings got in the way, and we decided we would take him home and nurse him back to health, thinking it was just a nervous breakdown.

The months that followed were a never-ending nightmare. As each day passed, he became more of a stranger, and his stares would send shivers up my spine. His constant pacing back and forth exhausted us as much as it did him, and then he would turn to sleep and complete isolation. We realized we had made a mistake in not having him admitted at the time of his first break, and now we had difficulty getting help. The police said there was nothing they could do because of the law. We didn't know where to turn.

Finally Danny took to the streets and would stare for hours on end in front of someone's home. Frightened neighbors began to complain. The police were besieged with calls, and they would pick him up and bring him home. One day I received a message to call the Chief of Police, who wanted to know what was going on. We spoke for about 10 minutes. The next time the police dropped off my son I began to shake as I went out to speak with them. I told them I had heard the neighbors were going to file a complaint against the Police Department. This was not true; I guess I lied out of desperation. Whatever the reason, it seemed to do the trick. The next time the police picked up Danny they brought him to a medical center for evaluation. He was then admitted to a state hospital, much to our relief. It was the beginning of many admissions and discharges, a span of eight years, causing us to constantly swing between hope and despair. He would do well in the hospital and then, once discharged, it would be about three or four months before he deteriorated, causing another hospitalization.

We are finally facing the sad fact that this is the way it is.

The world can be frightening to schizophrenics. At times they see things differently than normal people do. Some see people and objects weird and misshapen. When this happens, patients become frightened and back away, sometimes screaming uncontrollably. It is understandable. They are seeing a nightmare. Most schizophrenics are unable to concentrate or communicate without a great deal of difficulty. Often what they say makes no sense to the person listening. Patients may be hearing voices telling them what or what not to do. This is frightening to the families. Some patients become so frightened at what they see and hear that they want to go back to the hospital.

One day when I was visiting Jean, she suddenly looked at me strangely and backed away, frightened. We had been having a pleasant visit so I felt I could ask her what had happened.

"Jean, why are you looking at me like that? You look like you're frightened to death of me."

"You don't look right to me. You don't look like my mother. You look like an Egyptian mummy," she said. "You frighten me."

"Do I always look like a mummy to you?"

"No," Jean said. "Only sometimes."

Hearing this, I felt better because I understood what was happening. Since her response was so good, I decided to ask her about "her voices." She told me she still hears voices, and she seemed to think everyone hears them. Even so, the voices are very frightening to her. Jean also said she sometimes sees hands floating in the air.

I explained to her this was all part of her illness, and when these things happen, she should try not to get upset because they would go away in a little while. "Try not to be afraid," I told her.

Since I talked to Jean about this she seems to understand her situation a little more and is coping a little better. To prevent scenes, I leave now when I see that look in her eyes, knowing that I'm changing in front of her. Usually she calls me later and tells me she's sorry she acted so frightened.

It is necessary for parents to try to understand the behavior of their sons or daughters, to realize that chronic mental illness is a real sickness that manifests itself in many ways and to try to recognize signs that point to changes, good or bad. Though it is difficult to accept during the first years of the illness, parents must also realize that even when the patients are considered well enough to go into the community for outpatient programs, it does not necessarily mean there will be clear sailing to stabilization. It is, in fact, most likely that there will be a long period of trial and error as various outpatient programs are tried until an effective set of circumstances is found for the individual.

It has been a long road from Jean's first discharge from the hospital. We had been so happy then because her condition seemed greatly improved.

She appeared glad to be home. Arrangements were made for her to enter a "day hospital" program, which is a structured daycare center that does not provide overnight facilities. She would attend this program for three months, with the staff helping her to cope so that eventually she could hold a job.

A compassionate counselor from the daycare center came to our home to inform Jean about the program but she was not interested in it. We assumed she was afraid to attempt anything new. The counselor told her she was under no obligation to attend the program. That upset her father and me as we desperately wanted help for her. We didn't say anything but we wondered what this man was trying to do. As it turned out, he used reverse psychology on Jean, and it worked. Though Jean refused to go at first, she finally said she would give it a try. Her father escorted her there on the first day, and after one hour, she said she might enjoy it.

Jean attended the program for three months and did well, considering her condition. The staff then started her on a job in the housekeeping department at a local hotel but she was unable to handle this responsibility. In fact, she was not in any condition to work. Her counselor apparently had not realized Jean couldn't concentrate on anything for any length of time.

It was finally agreed that Jean would do better working in a "sheltered workshop" program a few days a week. In the program finally set up she worked at the sheltered workshop two days a week and went to the community drop-in center three days a week. Because she was unable to sit still at work, her counselor made arrangements for her to work for 15-minute periods. Under this schedule, she did well for a short time.

Families must learn to accept setbacks. If they are few and far between, that is cause for gratitude. But for the long-term mentally ill setbacks are more apt to be fairly frequent. Whether this is because of the treatment or because of the illness itself has yet to be determined. For the most part, under the present system of care and the state of research, parents can expect their sons and daughters who are chronically mentally ill to return again and again to a hospital for treatment or respite.

Though we were pleased with Jean's participation in an outpatient program, she still had setbacks. She would scream hysterically, claiming that people were trying to kill her. She held her hands over her head as if to protect herself from something seen only by her. She would calm down for a while, then again start screaming.

One particular time proved to be a terrible experience for her and for us. On a hot summer day, after being told not to go too far from home, she rode her bicycle swiftly for about a mile. She became tired and panicky because she had gone so far. She felt one of her spells coming on. Seemingly unaware of what she was doing, she ran screaming uncontrollably into the local YMCA and jumped into the deep end of the swimming pool. The swimmers didn't understand her behavior but one of them was smart enough to call the police.

When the police arrived, Jean became even more upset at the sight of the uniforms.

In another incident, our family went on a summer vacation to Florida. Jean was behaving well and wanted to go to Disneyland. As we were about to get on one of the amusement rides, she had an attack. We went a short distance on one of the cars but then had to ask if it could be stopped. We got off and brought her back to our car. Our relatives, who were with us, couldn't believe that this was their lovely niece screaming and swearing at us for three straight hours. When she calmed down, she said she was sorry. We later decided it was the large crowds of people and the hot weather that set her off. Now we were starting to understand what triggers Jean's outbursts.

When eventually she was sent to a state hospital, it was one of the worst days of our lives. It was a rough decision to send her to a place we knew little about. But we were told by professionals that it would be the best thing for her and us because her outbursts would continue and would disrupt the family. We were unable to cope with her violent behavior. Now she would be taken care of by professionals who could possibly help her.

Jean, after some improvement, was moved to a quarter-way house on the grounds of the state hospital, and at this writing she is living at a community residence in our home-town, doing quite well.

Tension builds up as parents wonder if in-and-out-of-the-hospital will happen again and again. Before becoming worn out physically, mentally and spiritually, mothers and fathers should take stock of themselves to become aware of their own limitations and breaking points. They often reach one of three positions—they acknowledge the hard facts, or they begin to think it would be easier to just die, or they begin to have horrible, guilt-ridden thoughts about how best to save themselves. Ideas of running away, of hiding somewhere, of checking on the welfare of a son or daughter somehow from a distance become an escape thought pattern that, of course, adds to the parents' guilt. But in their hearts, most parents know they cannot, will not, abandon their mentally ill child.

Even under normal helpful conditions, a mentally ill child is so fragile he or she is unable to function without support. When that person runs away, to parts unknown, his situation becomes more precarious, and the family suffers deeper, more unbearable pain.

Families need to find support from every possible avenue, to reach out for help from such agencies as the police, the department of mental health, and the Salvation Army, which maintains a missing persons bureau. The Salvation Army circulates information and photographs to all possible areas of help, and this service is provided free of charge, saving the family from additional financial burden.

All days are sad but some are filled with more anguish than others. One time in particular was when Danny left the state (he was not living at home during this period) to go to California. He was not ill, he said, and would start over elsewhere "since this town is sick." He had attempted a long journey once before, with awful results, but that did not deter him. Earlier he had used public transportation but now he planned to hitchhike.

Since at that time I was able to comprehend very little of what he did or said, I just shrugged my shoulders and said, "Oh, well," as my whole body went numb. I guess the giving in keeps us sane.

The days were long and painful while he was gone. There was not one word from him but somehow I was able to survive the daytime since light gave me hope and made everything seem safe. But the nights—oh, how I dreaded the nights. I was so consumed with fears for my son that it was impossible to sleep. As soon as I closed my eyes I would see him running on the highway, to the point of exhaustion. His clothes would be tattered and dirty. He was hungry and cold and couldn't even realize it. I constantly saw a lonely, pitiful figure, walking the earth in total isolation. I would also see him running in the woods, lost, as voices haunted him. Suddenly tears were streaming down his face as his fright took over. So much more I saw, and then at various times throughout the night, when my own fright took over, I would sit upright in my bed and cry out his name.

This went on for over a month before we received a call from a priest in California, and arrangements were made to bring Danny back. He came home looking like a prisoner of war held under extremely cruel conditions.

After another much too brief hospitalization, he came home to live. During this period Danny was unable to function. Then one evening he began to pace frantically around the house and in an agitated voice began to tell me that when he went to California, he would run so fast that he would vomit, and then a woman would sing to him to make him happy. I now knew that what I had feared truly happened, and as my own horrible nightly scenes flashed before me, I quickly reached out to embrace him, wishing with all my heart and soul that I could remove all of his suffering . . . forever.

If, with the advice and support of professionals and friends, parents decide not to have the ill member live at home, the decision must be made absolutely clear to the son or daughter. There can be no wavering, no giving in that allows the child to "come home for a while." There can be occasional visits for a few hours or a day, overnight visits for one or two nights but no move toward a permanent home arrangement. It would only cause prolonged suffering for the parents and child.

Fears of the ill member banging on the door in the middle of the night, of waking the neighbors, of a complaint to the police—these will be overcome if parents have the fortitude to enforce their decision. It's hard but it can be done. No parent wants to tell his sick child he or she cannot come home to stay. Many never do say it but manage to arrange that situation without hurting the son or daughter. It is hard, and it is heartbreaking, to exercise that kind of fortitude but it is done for the good of the patient.

Most of the long-term mentally ill hold on desperately to the hope that eventually they will be able to go home to live with their families. This hope often causes them to turn their backs on proper treatment or refuse to accept their illness. When parents feel enveloped in guilt, when they feel that they are abandoning their children by not letting them come home to stay, then parents should realize that actually they are helping their children to stand on their own, with support from professionals, so that they can survive when the parents pass away.

So many times on a rainy night, I think back to when I had to make one of the hardest decisions of my life.

Danny was absolutely stubborn about accepting help, about admitting to his illness or adjusting in any way, making his illness even more impossible to bear. I was completely at wit's end that day when he had been picked up by the police after routinely running away from the hospital. Brought back to the hospital, he was refused admission, according to the instructions of the department. The admitting persons said Danny had to understand that the hospital was not a hotel. They told me to stand firm and not allow him in the house, not even open the door. Because of the commitment laws, there was no other recourse.

I paced back and forth at home, knowing he would soon

be at the door—cold, wet, hungry and exhausted. In the past I always let him in, fed him, and brought him back to the hospital. How could I find the strength to say no to him? Wasn't it even against my religion, I thought. Mary never abandoned Jesus. What was I to do? Then I realized I had no choice, for it would be chaos if he lived at home. Well, I thought, if God was to damn me, so be it. And yet I knew if a tragedy befell my son that night because of my refusal to let him in, I would neither forgive nor be able to live with myself. I was so numb I couldn't even pray, but I knew I had to make a decision and stick to it if any benefit was to result from it.

As expected. he was now at my door. I couldn't tolerate the constant banging and opened the door slightly. Seeing his haggard face and pleading eyes reminded me of the time a few months earlier when he sat at the kitchen table begging me to let him live at home, crying, "Mom, I have already suffered more than Jesus!" I tried to keep my voice calm as I finally told him he had to leave, and the best thing he could do was go to the hospital and tell them he would take medicine and follow the program.

In between his leaving and coming back to pound on the door some more, I would think of the many times I saw on television sick people coming from various countries to the United States for special medical help, and they would receive transportation, cards, gifts, donations, all kinds of love pouring in, the royal treatment, as it should be. But for the mentally ill? They were treated like the lepers of long ago.

Somehow I got through the long night. Where Danny ended up I don't know, perhaps the woods or some abandoned place, trying to escape the elements. He was picked up by the police a few days later and admitted to the hospital, soon to be discharged again. He tried living in a room, took a job for a week, quit, back again to the hospital after a serious incident. Then, little by little, he began to accept help. I think he realizes he cannot make it on his own anymore. Danny still talks about his future at times, but not for long. We now visit him, take him out to dinner once a week, and he comes home for holidays.

I feel I am one of the lucky ones. Except for cruel suffering, Danny survived, and I'm still surviving. To date, I have not given up hope that things will get better. If I do, I have lost everything.

Chapter 3

How Brothers and Sisters See It

It is now evident that well siblings often experience emotional trauma when they have a schizophrenic sister or brother. Until very recently most research and counseling of family members have focused primarily on the parents as bearers of psychological trauma. Professional acknowledgment of the family's burden and emotional turmoil was often offset by the idea that the parents had contributed to causing schizophrenia, even if inadvertently.

Furthermore, it is natural for therapists to hear and attend to the loudest and neglect the quiet family members who express their needs less boldly or not at all. Also, siblings frequently withdraw from the family in order to cope with the stress they experience. Emotions such as anger, fear, shame, guilt, and depression are common. Major questions arise, such as, "Will I become mentally ill like[4] my brother or sister? Will my children become mentally ill?" Whether spoken or unspoken, conscious or unconscious, these serious concerns create an undertone of anxiety and insecurity. The survival-oriented responses siblings often make are to shut down parts of their emotional lives, to become overresponsible or to disengage from the ill member or the family as a whole. In light of these factors the problems of sisters and brothers have been frequently ignored—and so have their potential positive contributions to helping the family and the ill person cope with chronic mental illness.

Professionals who wish to help the family cope should remember that siblings tend to be an untapped resource. In fact, they can supply information from a unique perspective because their emotional involvement may be less intense than it is for parents. Because siblings tend to be overinvolved or underinvolved, they may be in a position to have a powerful effect on the family by altering their role—by taking an active role if they have been more peripheral or by becoming more distant if they've become overinvolved or "parentified." Parents, and even the ill sibling, may be able to "hear" information from a well sibling that is more difficult to accept from a professional. Such information may include insights about the limitations of the ill sibling or about the possibility of altering the roles that family members usually play, thereby enhancing the strengths and flexibility of the family.

It was with a desire to learn from these close relatives bonded by blood, as well as to provide them with information and counseling, that a monthly sibling group was begun by two professionals in a Massachusetts community. The group, some of whose members are children of the individuals writing this book, is part of a national trend toward bringing brothers and sisters of the mentally ill into groups where their feelings can be shared and understood. These siblings are making a very real contribution to the understanding of problems families share. In their new role as consultants to professionals rather than only counselees, siblings have written and spoken about a variety of topics, at first hesitantly and then with a sense of relief in being able to share their difficult, often painful experiences and emotions.

Together these stories provide much important information about the effect of mental illness on the family as a whole, as well as on sisters and brothers. More often than not, however, parents attempt to "protect" well siblings from the situation. They give such reasons as, "The illness has been going on for so long, it isn't necessary to stir up emotions all over again," or, "The other children have their own lives to lead, and I don't want to bother them with this."

A family may wish to preserve their "successful" children from "contagion," the feared harm that would result from too much contact with the mentally ill brother or sister. Despite its protective intentions, this course of action can lead to a lack of honest discussion of the painful feelings family members are experiencing, and this creates a further bind for siblings. Unable to talk about the range and intensity of emotions they feel, siblings may become stuck or "frozen" and unable to get on with their own lives. In these instances it is only when the feelings related to their brother's or sister's illness are acknowledged, accepted, and understood that siblings once again begin charting their own course in life. One brother who had moved from denial of his actual feelings to acceptance of them summed things up like this: "The parents probably think everything is fine. They don't realize one member's mental illness affects everyone else in the family."

For a variety of reasons one or more siblings are at times more able to come to terms with the reality of their brother's or sister's mental illness sooner than others in the family. When this is so, they may be able with gentleness and care help reduce the feelings of guilt and failure of other family members that often accompany this tragedy. Through open discussion the family can be helped to assess and use services outside the family, to realize the limits of family emotional resources and thereby more effectively care for the ill members.

Siblings who have taken part in the group have found it easier to accept and deal with their mentally ill brothers and sisters and to live their own lives after they have aired their feelings and had their unfamiliar emotions explained to them. Like many new and untried things in life, a sibling group may seem unnecessary but experience has proven it can be an essential asset to brothers and sisters of the mentally ill. The group is a consciousness-raising experience. In retrospect one sibling wrote, "Thank you for allowing me to express my feelings in a supportive, nonjudgmental atmosphere."

If someone had said to me during one of the family meetings we had for Anne that a group for brothers and sisters was available, I would have grabbed it. I thought those family meetings were for the entire family. I wanted something just for me. I was hurting so bad. It's been 10 long years.

Whether gradual or sudden, the appearance of the initial symptoms tends to elicit reactions of confusion, shock and upset. Siblings have their own individual views of mental illness when it first appears in a brother or sister.

I can vividly remember the first symptoms of Jean's illness several months before her complete breakdown, but at the time we couldn't make the connection. It was a time of both anger and concern over her unusual behavior. She appeared to be acting like a spoiled, rebellious brat. At the time of her first violent outburst, my initial reaction was one of confusion. I felt like punching her because of her physical and verbal abuse of my mother, but I was her brother, and I couldn't bring myself to do it. Yet, she had to be restrained from harming us. I had never experienced anything like this in my life.

A sister who shares a room with her stricken family member will see the breakdown from a more intimate angle.

Before they labeled Jean a schizophrenic, I noticed a change in her. She gave money away freely, bought lots of clothes she never wore, probably forgetting she had bought them, played one record continuously. She started crying and had nightmares frequently. Since we shared a room, she kept me up at nights, making my school grades go down. When she got worse, I was afraid to bring friends home to visit because she became upset very easily, and she would upset everyone at home. When she started her outbursts, I would walk as far as I could to get away from her because I thought more people around her would just prolong the outbursts.

Conclusions may be drawn without adequate basis in fact. As one brother put it, these thoughts can "have no real direction."

I think that no matter how much you analyze someone's past history, you still won't be able to say he'll have mental illness. I thought Peter's behavior was strange, but I just put it down to a different type of lifestyle, and no matter how much everyone else said they saw "something" coming, I believe that no one had any prescience on the matter of his mental illness.

At times there is violence in the home; almost certainly there is a disruption of "family life as usual." When mental illness leads to violence in the family, a brother or sister can feel fearful and vulnerable. The bond of trust that was taken for granted is broken.

Just before Peter was admitted to the hospital I was scared to death after hearing him upstairs talking to himself. I didn't know what to do or say or think. I told our brother Buddy. He said, "I know. I heard him." But he didn't care to talk about it so neither did I. Then one incident happened I will never forget.

I was doing the dishes, talking on the phone with a

friend. Suddenly Peter came up behind me and hit me hard on the back of my neck with a fist. I turned around. He started laughing and ran up to his room. I was in total shock. I couldn't speak. I hung up the phone and sat down, shaking uncontrollably. Mom and Dad were in the other room but I didn't dare tell them because I didn't know what they'd do to Peter. I went up in my room and just cried. I couldn't understand him or why he did it but I've never confronted him with it. I told Mom a few days later but she said nothing to Peter.

The first hospitalization of a family member signals the family's entry into a new world of mental hospitals and mental health professionals. Even though the ill sibling may have been involved with psychiatrists and other helping professionals before, the initial hospitalization, particularly to a locked ward, can be most disturbing to the brother or sister of the ill person. Usually, they do not understand mental illness. In addition, the experience of being "locked in" to the ward when visiting often inspires fear. Other patients may appear bizarre, out of touch, dangerous, frightening. The well family member often becomes anxious about the welfare of his or her brother or sister, who is surrounded by these "others." The well siblings may for the first time wonder if this will be their fate—to go crazy and be locked away. Also, there can be many mixed feelings concerning the justice or injustice of involuntary hospitalization. The mental health system can be seen as one of oppression and incarceration rather than of healing and nurturing. And seeing one's own brother or sister sedated on heavy doses of medication, and often disoriented, tends to evoke concern, sorrow, and feelings of helplessness.

I found hospital visits to be very disturbing for a long time. I didn't know what was wrong with these people. I didn't understand the side effects from the medications. I worried a lot, wondering if this could happen to me. I got scared every time I went there and had doors locked behind me.

Another thing that bothered the hell out of me was sitting in the lobby having a visit with my sister Anne when a new patient would be brought in by an ambulance. To me it was such a dramatic moment to see these new patients, so innocent and helpless, with those restraints on their wrists, being brought in against their will. I couldn't even look. That sight would stay in my mind for a long time. For a while I thought every ambulance I saw on the street was forcibly taking someone to a mental hospital.

I often dreamed about Anne. Often it would be that she was a very healthy, happy, normal person. Sometimes it would be about her running away from the hospital. Sometimes I dreamed she was free and I was her in the hospital and I would always run away.

Seeing one's own relative sedated on heavy doses of medication and often disoriented tends to evoke concern and feelings of sorrow. It is easy to feel that an ill brother or sister is a stranger.

I was greatly put off by Peter's drooling, the blank facial expression, and the tiredness all the time. He really looked and acted like he was mentally retarded. It took me a long time to realize it was just the medication, that Peter was still Peter.

A family's self-image may be shaken to the core by the event of hospitalization. Given the stigma of mental illness and the public's vast misinformation about it, people in the family may feel "tainted" and ashamed. Siblings who often are both connected to and yet outside of the ill person's dilemma can be profoudly affected by these difficult emotional currents within the family. Suddenly the tide shifts and family members do not know what to say or what to do. Feelings of helplessness and confusion then become companions of brothers and sisters as well as patients and parents.

I think we all knew, to some degree, that my brother Peter had a few problems, especially after he came back from his stint at school. However, an attitude of "everyone has problems" and "this too shall pass" was pretty much adopted. Betty, Aline, and Cathy, our older sisters, were leading independent lives away from home when he went into the hospital. It was a great shock to them. Initial feelings ran the gamut from "poor Peter" to "how could this happen to one of us?" As a family it shook us. For days it was averted glances and nervous talk among us, as though we were afraid that if we did or said something wrong, it would be taken the wrong way by somebody else.

When Peter first went into the hospital, it was, needless to say, a shock to everyone. I don't think anyone has really been the same since. I think that everyone in the family, to some degree and for some amount of time, felt some fear or disgust when Peter went into the hospital, no matter what they say now. To think that one of our family had a mental illness and had to go into the hospital was odious. It never reached the point where anyone tried to hush it up but the feeling was definitely there. Eventually, I think, we all gave up such thoughts and became supportive of Peter. One thing is for sure, our family was changed permanently in a way I can't put my finger on.

The time of first hospitalization may be the well siblings' first extended contact with mental health professionals. While this can be a positive, clarifying, reassuring experience, many very often find it is not. They feel the family is being "studied" or "scrutinized" in family meetings. While professionals may not intend to blame the family for causing the illness, their questions and observations may be taken as such by family members already feeling guilty, ashamed, or confused. And the reality is that some professionals do blame family members for causing or contributing to the illness. Other mental health workers, such as ward attendants, are often overworked and underpaid. Family members can feel that the ill person is not receiving the quality of care he or she deserves. Feelings of being intimidated by doctors, social workers, and psychologists are also common. And brothers and sisters often feel their needs are being ignored as the professionals' attention becomes focused on the patient.

> *The conference was* held in a large room with most of my family seated in a semicircle and a psychiatrist facing us. Behind the doctor were roughly eight to ten counselors and case coordinators. We were all introduced to each of them but really had no idea why they were there. It was a most uncomfortable feeling. It seemed as though I was a guinea pig in a cage being scrutinized in every way with each word I spoke. What made things worse was the doctor who asked each of us different questions. Just by the questions it seemed as though he really didn't know what was going on with Peter. To me, the others seemed disinterested. Now that I look back I'm not really sure if they were or if I was the one who was feeling disinterested with the whole meeting. Nonetheless this is how I felt at the time.
>
> I didn't want to answer any of the doctor's questions except with one word answers because I didn't want him or the other people looking on knowing every detail about our family. I really didn't think they cared as much about our problems as we did. I also really didn't think any of these people could help Peter.
>
> I felt as though I gained nothing from this experience.

I received a totally negative image of psychiatrists and counselors.

Certainly some families have positive experiences with
professionals. A family can appreciate the dedication of
professionals and want to work more closely with them but
not know how. Even when attitudes about professionals
are positive, there are often mixed feelings concerning
family-professional cooperation.

During the past 10 years of Anne's illness, I don't recall
one bad experience with any of the professionals my family
and I have had to deal with. I have found the social workers
at the hospital to be very nice people. They didn't always
volunteer information but if I asked them anything, they
were great about explaining things to me. I've always been
impressed with their patience, understanding, knowledge,
insight, and sincerity.

I think of all the verbal abuse I've seen the social workers take from Anne. Also, there is the abuse I've heard about
and the abuse I can imagine but have not heard about. I can
appreciate what professionals go through. I think of the times
I spent all night in the emergency room and how the mental
health workers would be on a phone for hours trying to find
a facility with an extra bed or making arrangements for her
to go to Westboro State Hospital. They were always kind
and were very careful to make the right decisions as to what
treatment they thought was best for her.

It often made me mad that my sister couldn't appreciate what good people she had to work with. I really believe
they tried very hard to help her. At times they were all Anne
really had, the only human contact she had. It is a pity she
doesn't trust them enough and fights them instead.

One regret I have is that I didn't work closer with the
social workers for my sister's sake as well as my own. The
family meetings inhibited me a great deal. I don't feel at all

comfortable discussing issues I think are important if it means
members of the family may become hurt or defensive about
what I have to say.

I think one-on-one meetings are more honest and
accomplish a lot more as far as gathering information about
the family relationship. I think the family meetings are very
important for other reasons, such as to show and offer support and discuss things that don't upset anyone.

Just as there are skilled and unskilled workers in every
field, so there are mental health professionals with varying
degrees of competence. Lay persons often find this reality
confusing due to their tendency to treat professionals with
respect and even with awe.

My first experience with a mental health professional was
with a well-known psychiatrist who was treating my sister
Jean at the onset of her illness. He seemed to be arrogant
and cold, more concerned with receiving his next $75 than
with helping my sister. Most psychiatrists are probably very
dedicated people.

After a year of disappointing episodes with the psychiatrist, we placed Jean in a community mental health program. The dedicated young professionals there took a
genuine and sincere interest in her illness. Their salary is
much less than a psychiatrist's but I believe they are just as,
if not more, effective. We had several family meetings with
them, and they really helped us to cope with and understand her schizophrenia. Now that she is living in a group
home they are still very much in contact with us. Every community should have this type of family support.

Siblings of mentally ill people do, of course, have feelings, many of which are difficult to bear and more difficult
to understand. Guilt over his or her own well-being is common. Those whose lives are moving ahead and providing

them with some success and satisfaction often silently wonder, "Why me? Why is my life going well while my sister's is in chaos? Does enjoying my life while she suffers this tragic illness make me a bad person?" These sorts of thoughts may be denied and unconscious. If so, the well siblings may find various physical or emotional problems cropping up in other parts of their lives. In cases where this agonizing recognition is faced, the well young family members ask themselves or others exactly what is owed to the ill family member. They ask, "What are my family obligations to my sister?" "Should I be my brother's keeper?"

> *Leaving the hospital* was always a relief but I also felt sad leaving Anne behind. I felt guilty for being happy in my life while my sister was so unhappy. I didn't feel right having a good time when she couldn't. I felt guilty if I wasn't always thinking of her.

Brothers and sisters often wonder if they somehow caused the illness or failed to spot the early warnings and prevent it. The healthy siblings may have guilt about resentment they feel toward the ill person for disrupting family life and adding stress to their lives. As feelings of envy or jealousy surface in response to the increased attention paid by relatives to the ill person, guilt may appear due to continuing feelings of sibling rivalry. Finally, there may be guilt about not feeling guilty enough. That is, the well brothers and sisters may punish or chastise themselves for not caring or for establishing a distance from the situation, a distance that may often be needed.

> *After I went to* see Peter a few times, I began to feel guilty for a variety of reasons. First and foremost I deeply regretted my resentment. I realized how foolish I had been to think Peter became ill on purpose just to screw me up. Seeing

him in the hospital, I began to see how far beyond his control it was at the time. Also, the way he expressed his concern over my prom and graduation showed me how guilty he himself must have felt.

To a much lesser degree, I felt guilty over the fact that perhaps I had helped cause his illness by the way I treated him. He had always treated me in a somewhat offhanded way, as most older brothers would treat younger ones, but to a greater degree I was somewhat cocky to him. I think our antagonism was a bit overblown on both sides. Actually, in thinking about it, I felt more guilty over the fact that I didn't feel guilty enough. It was at this time we had these family interviews with professionals, and it was during those that most everyone said that they felt somewhat guilty about helping along Peter's illness.

Anger is as common as guilt. There can be anger at the loss of a valued companion and confidant, anger at having to assume more responsibility within the family, anger because there is much frustration and no easy answers, anger at guilt feelings disrupting peace of mind, anger about the sense of powerlessness one feels in helping the ill brother or sister, anger at the unfairness of it all.

For my sister and me it was a major and busy part of our lives at the time Peter first went into the hospital. School was winding down, and we were about to graduate. The class trip and the prom were coming up. When Peter went into the hospital, it sort of froze me in mid-step. As Peter's younger brother, my initial shock gave way to sympathy. Then, as the days wore on, I began to change in my demeanor. Every day someone went to visit Peter, twice a day. In all honesty, I began to resent this because I felt as though I was being drained by his illness, along with everyone else in the family. It didn't seem fair to me, at the time, that at one of the major junctures in my life Peter would "screw it up." The feeling of resentment became very strong, although I let no one know about it, least of all Peter.

Anger may be directed toward family members, toward oneself or toward the ill member. One may feel judgmental toward other family members for the way they are handling the illness or toward oneself for the same reason. There is likely to be annoyance at the ill family member for real or imagined offenses, which may include violence.

One thing that really bothered me was Mom's overprotectiveness, especially when Peter came home from the hospital. She would let Peter have anything and say anything. She told us specifically not to get him upset. "Just act like yourselves," she said. Fine and good. But every time I'd be reading or watching TV she'd say, "Why don't you go and talk to Peter or play ball or do something with him? You're his sister." I got really angry. If he wanted to, he'd ask me. I tried to tell her but it would go in one ear and out the other. She'd make all his favorite meals, and he'd never have to wash dishes or do a single chore around the house.
Sometimes I don't think Peter wants to help himself. He seems to let everyone else do the worrying for him— what he's going to do, where he's headed. He's just content to sit back and live at home here and have not a care in the world. I suppose that's what rubs me the wrong way about Peter. He's got so much to offer but he does nothing with it.

Another common aspect of sibling stress is a feeling of embarrassment or humiliation as they try to include their brother or sister in social events either within or outside the family. The drama unfolds something like this: Feeling "different," the mentally ill sibling (either before or after the illness is diagnosed) acts in unusual ways. Yet there is a corresponding need to assert that nothing is wrong with him or her as a person. Feeling profoundly unstable, he compensates by rigidly insisting that all he does is right, that he has "every right" to be different. What seems like willful opposition can be combined with a true inability to see things from another point of view and a desperate wish to hold on to a sense of identity. Whether a nonconformist by temperament or not, the ill person wishes at the deepest level to be accepted by others as a peer, a competent equal. However, the denial of the extremely painful reality of one's own mental instability has its consequences.

The mentally ill person frequently alienates those whose acceptance he craves. While appearing to be self-absorbed and socially out of touch, he is just as often feeling increasingly terrified, enraged, hopeless or helpless about others' rejection of him, rejection he is often helping to create. For the well sibling, the wish to support and include his brother or sister is commonly mixed with a sense of confused loyalties and social discomfort. A sibling asks himself or herself, "What will my friends / lover think of me when they find out?"

> *Peter is very* independent. He believes he is right, and he doesn't like making concessions to other people. He doesn't like conforming, and I believe he derives great pleasure in being different to a great degree. This makes it very hard for me when I ask him to go out, either just the two of us or with some of my friends. When he does something strange (antisocial), it is embarrassing to me and to Peter, too. But he can't help it.
>
> The only comparison I can make is with an uncoordinated athlete playing ball with good players. Peter's attitude won't allow him to admit to himself that he is uncoordinated and act accordingly so he goes banging through the game awkwardly, which not only upsets the other players and makes

them want him to leave but also hurts him because he can't understand why they aren't playing his type of game.

While a certain amount of depression is inevitable in facing the tragedy of mental illness, these feelings can become pathological and chronic. When sadness, anger or hopelessness are not expressed and confronted, the result is more pain. In discussing the sense of mourning, which was quite bitter, one sister said, "The Jackie we knew is dead." Another said, "There are times when I feel that my sister would be better off dead." If anger is not expressed, as is often the case, depression can become a constant state of mind for the well sibling.

> *I really became* quite depressed most of the time. I don't know why but I really let the thing get to me. I felt like I was mourning a death, and I wasn't going to stop mourning.

This sorrow may be related to the brothers' or sisters' inability to help their sibling or to the loss of the sister or brother relationship that used to be or to their difficulty in comforting other well family members (who may be reluctant to show their real feelings, wishing to appear strong).

> *Every time I* see Jean it hurts me. It hurts me because I feel helpless and because I cannot do anything for her. Every time I look at her I think, "What if she wasn't so sick?" I see how her mind has deteriorated, and I see how forgetful she is. I still love her but she is a different person in my sister's body. It is as if she is dead but her body is still functioning. If she were sick some other way or handicapped, I could still communicate with her if her mind was functioning, but because of her sickness I can't reach her old self. Sometimes I wish I could put our past relationship out of my mind so

when I see her now, it wouldn't hurt me so much.

I've accepted the fact that she will never be the same again, but it is still so very painful to see her. When people say she is making progress, even small amounts, that gives me hope that she is getting better but I see her more often as regressing.

I wondered why I was close to tears when certain stabbing recollections came up. I guess it was because it hurts to see another in confusion where you can only stand by and watch, helpless to do or say anything to lessen it. Even now a pinch of anxiety and uneasiness comes to me, just thinking about it.

Catastrophic fears and pessimistic expectations about the future can easily fill the void opened by loss and mourning. A journal or diary can be a helpful vehicle in expressing emotions and confronting them.

I'm glad I decided to start a journal. It helps me think more clearly. Why is Peter in the hospital? He's sicker than I ever thought. And Mom and Dad all wicked upset. Mom goes into coughing fits and has backaches; Dad almost had a diabetic reaction. A sickening thought hit me. What about rape? Could it come to that? It scares me. Will he be in and out of the hospital for the rest of his life? Nobody knows what's going on in Peter's mind. I don't think anyone knows what's happening, not even Peter. He's more screwed up than we all recognized. I think he's afraid of being found out. Makes me feel lost.

Brothers and sisters eventually gain perspective as they reexamine the past and present, fantasize about the future, and look more deeply into their experiences.

Maybe Peter's sick of seeing everyone else leave and "make it," and he feels inferior or maybe incapable somehow. As his sister, it seemed strange to me that whenever someone came in when I was talking with Peter, he'd stop talking and go upstairs. Whenever friends came over, he'd make himself invisible until they left. I asked him why. He just said he didn't like crowds and left it at that.

As I look back, I realize Peter always made me uneasy for some reason. His fits of rage and quickness to lash out really scared me. Even during play fighting, playing games, just fooling around in the backyard, he was intense in his emotions. I could never sit down and just talk with him. Conversation always seemed strained.

The increased introspection that brothers and sisters go through may be painful but eventually rewarding. One sister noted that if the search is only for blame, it will certainly be painful. But in the long run, honest introspection by the well sibling will deepen understanding of both himself or herself and the ill member.

I clearly recall that when Peter went into the hospital, I thought to myself his aggressive pattern of behavior when younger was uncommon but that this in itself proved nothing. You must understand that my brother and sister and I also participated in these strange games—such as crashing our bicycles into each other, almost enjoying the violence. I thought it over again, however, and one thing struck me. Peter never showed any remorse for any of his actions. He did in fact seem belligerently nonapologetic.

Brothers and sisters have a unique story to tell about the effect of mental illness on the family as a whole and specifically about *their* relationships with various family members. For example, their relationships with parents can easily become strained as each manifests the stress of coping with chronic illness in the family. Confusion can cloud communications, particularly soon after the illness has appeared. Contradictions may invade the day-to-day conversations of the family. Well-meaning parents may say the equivalent of: "Be close to your sister. Give her lots of space. Don't give up hope. She may get well, and we hope she does. Hope but don't expect the best. It's a chronic illness but encourage her when you see her."

> *When talking to* Mom about Peter's illness, it was very exasperating for several reasons. She always talked at us, never with us. She seemed to ramble on in a way without ever really saying much. Also, she seemed not to really know exactly what she was talking about, which made it seem all the more useless.
>
> The most annoying thing, however, was how she explained that it was no one's fault but how it really was everyone's fault, and how we should all pay a lot of attention to Peter. This was so aggravating because at the time I felt little at fault, that what happened was his problem. I also felt that I had my own life to live, and he had his, and never the two shall meet.

The illness may accentuate and bring to the fore splits within the family which existed before the illness ever became apparent. Rage and hatred can surface and create even greater rifts between family members. Family members at times "scapegoat" the patient—ignoring him, distancing themselves, or mocking the patient and any family member who tries to help him. In families where there is much unexpressed anger and resentment, father, mother, brothers, sisters and other relatives may find themselves taking sides "for" or "against" the ill member.

> *If I were* in Anne's position, I couldn't stand the thought of the whole family turning away from me. Anne can't understand why her brothers and sisters won't come to see

her. She calls them on the phone. No one calls her. I hate
hearing her own family put her down, her brothers and sisters laughing as they tell stories about her. Why won't the
others give a little? Anne is so hurt.

In other settings, healthy brothers and sisters may for
the first time behold the frailty and vulnerability of their
parents. The revelation of parents' humanness in facing
tragedy and pain can be both disturbing and enlightening.
Suddenly parents can be seen in a more objective light as
"persons in their own right." For one sibling such an experience will be unnerving and a cause for upset and disap-
pointment, while for another the experience will lead to
deeper communication and closeness with the parents.

My mother, in my eyes, seemed vulnerable and almost
not able to cope. She seemed to be on the verge of a nervous
breakdown. It was for this reason that everyone endured
her "lectures." Everyone humored her. Everyone was more
careful and considerate of her than they used to be.
My father, at first, seemed to roll with the punches. It
soon became evident, however, that Peter's illness had a deep
effect on him. It wasn't in any clear way that I saw this but
rather I tried to read into his words and actions. Yet I couldn't
really talk to him about Peter because he was still "Dad." It
was a little ridiculous, too, because he still *acted* as though
Peter's illness didn't bother him even though everyone knew
it did. So, all in all, my views of my parents changed quite a
bit. They changed only a little as people but my perception
of them changed a lot. If I had to sum it up in a phrase, I
would say I can be a lot more comfortable, perhaps familiar,
with both of them now.

At times the experience of family pain helps to break
through patterns of fixed attitudes and ways of acting.
While, as noted earlier, this pain may lead to more dis-
couragement and bitterness, it can also lead to positive

changes. For instance, brothers and sisters writing for this book found that in facing the pain and their family problems, they often were able to see encouraging positive aspects in themselves and other family members, aspects brought to the fore through this searing experience. For such fortunate families there can be an increase in awareness and sensitivity toward others.

> *Although Jean's condition* was and still is a tremendous blow to our family, several noticeable positive changes have occurred for us.
>
> The most obvious change is in my parents. They are involved very actively with a local mental health organization, the Alliance for the Mentally Ill, which has aided many families of psychiatric patients who had nowhere to turn for advice, comfort, and valuable information that is not generally available to the public. Before this my parents were not involved with any organizations. I believe their new involvement is a great source of satisfaction for them. They've made many new friends of various backgrounds, and they all work well together.
>
> As for myself and my other sister, we have become much more aware of the problems of the mentally ill and their families. We have participated in writing some of our experiences about our sister's illness for this book so that others with similar problems need not feel guilty or ashamed over their family member's misfortune.
>
> I believe the family as a whole has become much closer since Jean's illness. We often discuss the problems of the mentally ill and their relatives and new legislation being proposed to help them. All in all, I feel that we've all become more compassionate people in the last several years. Sometimes it takes a tragedy such as this to bring it out.

These positive changes can be manifested as an increased ability to accept others as they are or a sense of being more receptive to others, of being able to "listen" to others more fully. A new sense of compassion for others' suffering can arise both within and outside the family. This may lead to the desire to contribute to the lives of others, as the brothers and sisters who have written for this book have done.

There have been changes in our family and changes in myself. It's just really hard to express these changes and even harder to say how I feel about them. First and foremost, I guess, is a new feeling of tension which seems to be around. I don't mean to say this is all negative tension, but some of it is. I guess it's a kind of paranoia about ourselves, about Peter or about our individual relationships, which become awkward at times. You don't know when or how far to push or when to back off. It gets scary at times, as though you have to monitor every syllable that comes out of your mouth. I have to qualify these statements by saying that this is how I perceived things at the time Peter was in the hospital, before he came home to live.

Over the long run, things have changed in a more permanent way. Everyone in our family seems to have gotten over the initial shock of Peter's hospitalization. Everyone now accepts things as the way they are, that it's no one's fault. With this acceptance has come a certain kind of maturity, a maturity that few are fortunate enough to get. It's the realization that life is not all wine and roses, that everyone has something wrong with him, that it doesn't only "happen to somebody else." In particular we learned that the term "mental illness" shouldn't be a stigma—that if not reversible, it is treatable. We've also come to accept Peter as a person, as a member of the family. Before, I think, it was, "Well, everyone's all right except Peter who has mental illness."

More than this, however, I think we've all become a lot more honest and feeling in our relationships with each other. If nothing more, this has taught us that we all have feelings and don't have to be embarrassed about them. I guess, to sum it up, we've become a more open family. I hesitate to say "closer" because I don't think we've achieved that.

Personally, I've changed a lot. What I've noticed most is a heightened awareness of other people around me. I think I've become more responsive to their feelings, more receptive to them. I find myself listening more and more and talking less and less. It's as though I realize there's a whole world out there with a million different stories to be told. This comes out of the awareness that people do have problems, and a lot of the time they only want someone to listen. I think of Peter and wonder what if only someone had sat down and listened to him.

I've also become a lot less judgmental of other people. I guess, too, that I've become a lot less self-centered through a heightened awareness of other people and their feelings. More than that, I guess it's an actual interest in other people, especially my family.

The realities of mental illness clearly are difficult to bear. Siblings remark that two qualities see them through this crisis faithfully: honesty, both with themselves and with other family members, and love, caring for others in the family while also caring for themselves. Along with knowledge about the illness, these are certainly powerful allies in negotiating one's way through this trial by fire.

To begin, I must first give a brief outline of my feelings for my brother Danny since I was a little girl. When I was very young, through elementary school and part of junior high, I know I looked up to my brother as being the oldest and smartest. I envied him his talent in drawing. One of my happiest times with him was when he helped me draw pictures of buildings at the desk in his room. I remember how thrilled I was at his attention.

Later on in my junior high years my brother treated

me as if he hated me, and I remember feeling confused and hurt but I still loved him. This went on for a couple of years. Then he moved, and I didn't see him until I was around 18. I couldn't believe the night I came home and he surprised me in the livingroom. He jumped up and gave me a hug and a kiss, and I remember being shocked but very happy. We started to talk, and he seemed to like me and things between us went well.

After about a year Danny was in a state hospital, and I couldn't understand why or how, and I was angry that it happened. I felt cheated.

It was also hard to see him act so irrationally, and at times I wanted to yell at him and shake him back into the real world. I couldn't accept the fact that it isn't that way and that he may be like this the rest of his life. I'm learning to accept his illness, and I know the most important thing will never change—I love him. He's my brother.

Chapter 4

The Rights and Wrongs of Patients' Rights

In spite of scientific advancement in treatment of various illnesses, the treatment for chronic mental illness has fallen behind, in great part because of existing laws. The greatest detriment to the mentally ill may be the "patients' rights" laws.

A most dangerous roadblock has been created by the civil libertarians in the treatment of the mentally ill though their intentions to help the patients were humane. They believe patients should be involved in matters concerning their treatment and their welfare. However, as parents know, in most cases the chronically mentally ill are unable to objectively make such decisions, and the families are in a helpless position as they stand by without the power to obtain treatment for their ill member.

Mental patients are human beings, and their rights must be respected. However, they are also sick, with an illness that affects their thinking. When they are in an acute state, they do not realize, nor do they understand, their limitations. At any given point, who is to say what is best for the patient? The patient, the parents, or the hospital staff?

Usually with medication most of the schizophrenic and

manic-depressive mentally ill can live a comparatively functional life. Why is it that with any other illness the family can seek help for their loved ones, but families of the mentally ill have to stand by helplessly while their loved one's condition is deteriorating? We get the continual response from the civil libertarians that we must remember the rights of the patient. Since many of the mentally ill do not admit to their illness, they see no need for medication, even though experience has shown that medication, in many instances, has been helpful.

While Legal Aid has many helpful as well as necessary functions, it has been most detrimental to my son Thomas. As he has an aversion to medication and believes he is not sick, he refuses medication. All he has to do is call his Legal Aid attorney, complain about having medication administered, and she will immediately block it. Of course, if medication is not given properly, it can have adverse results. However, when it is prescribed by a competent physician, with medication also prescribed to counteract side effects, it makes the difference between functioning and not functioning. Furthermore, my husband and I feel that medical decisions about treatment should be made only by the attending physician. Each patient should be considered individually to determine his or her condition—so that it is exactly known why it is necessary for the patient to have the medication. I feel strongly that it is a grave injustice for a Legal Aid lawyer to intervene in a physician's treatment. I think the law that provides for an attorney to defend his client's position, even to the patient's detriment, needs restudying.

In Thomas' case, without medication stresses build up to the extent that the agitation reaches such a high degree that he cannot function. Delusions of being harassed become constant, and he becomes most fearful—even if someone just looks in his direction. At this point, Thomas begins to run—north, west, south—in order to get away from the "harassment," unfortunately never admitting that it is because of his condition that he is going through such horrifying delusions.

Although professionals often tell families that their ill members are "survivors," it offers little comfort when parents see them in distressful situations in the community without support systems. It is incredible to the families that, for the most part, there is so little understanding by professionals, in all fields, and by laymen about the basic needs of the chronically mentally ill—which must include strong support systems. The very law that is supposedly protecting the rights of patients can, in fact, do them immeasurable harm.

At one point during Thomas' hospitalization when he was refusing medication and complaining more and more about being harassed and, of course, becoming more agitated, the doctor recommended that he be legally committed for a period so that it would be possible to treat him more effectively. A hearing before a judge was arranged, to take place at the hospital, and Thomas requested that his Legal Aid attorney be present. The lawyer negated the doctor's testimony when she presented some information in regard to Thomas' condition when he had been hospitalized some time in the past and had, at that time, shown some improvement. With this information, and in spite of Thomas' condition at the time, the judge—for some reason beyond the comprehension of my husband and myself—said, "I could commit him but I'm going to discharge him."

Needless to say, this was a most shocking conclusion to all of us who were interested in helping Thomas. Our concern reached a new peak. He had some money so we knew he would start traveling in order to run away from harassment and also to look for a school. School was his obsession.

He had been denied admission in a few schools because of his bizarre behavior.

Try to imagine a person in Thomas' condition taking to the road, encountering strangers along the way who couldn't be expected to understand his behavior. Imagine what might ensue if he were to accuse such people of harassing him. Right after the hearing, as we had feared, he left Massachusetts and kept running into harassment all the way. He registered for some courses in a few schools but left soon after for obvious reasons.

Thomas called me from many different towns, sounding most fearful, but refused to return to Massachusetts because the harassment was worse in Massachusetts, he said. He lived under some pretty bad conditions, we are sure, and kept running out of money. For a brief period that Thomas admitted to, he lived in a Salvation Army facility. He related that on one occasion a woman reported him to the police because, she said, he harassed her.

During all this time he did appeal to a few hospitals for help. After staying for a few days, he would insist on leaving. Finally, his condition worsened to the extent that he was not at all able to cope so he appealed to the FBI for help because he was being harassed, he told them. They in turn got in touch with the local mental health clinic. He was admitted to a general hospital and then transferred to a psychiatric hospital where he was committed for six months.

The doctor at the hospital, in contacting us, told me that Thomas' condition was poor when he was first admitted. Considering the condition that he was in, it was most fortunate that he did not run into a more serious outcome— but it was certainly bad enough. Had he remained in Massachusetts instead of being discharged after the hearing, his condition would have started to improve with treatment, but instead, with additional stresses, his condition deteriorated. The doctor also told me that, after having been at the hospital for a month, Thomas began to function somewhat.

Although he had been committed for six months, he

thought he was well enough to be discharged at the end of three months. While the doctor didn't feel that he had improved sufficiently, he felt that if Thomas was transferred to a board and care facility and attended a nearby clinic and continued with medication, he might get along. And so he was transferred—which proved to be unsatisfactory in every way. He left there after staying only a few days and decided to head back to Massachusetts. On the way he checked into a YMCA and found he couldn't function enough to even leave the room

With the kind assistance of the social worker on the staff of the hospital Thomas had left just a few days previously, who had worked with him during his hospitalization there, it was arranged for him to be transported to a hospital nearby, where he remained for two weeks. I traveled there and returned with him by plane. Back in Massachusetts, he was admitted to the psychiatric hospital he had left six months earlier. He had lost so much ground in that period. He has been in this hospital for six weeks now and is just beginning to function to a limited degree.

The stresses that kept building while Thomas was in transit for all those dangerous months left scars which will take a very long time to overcome.

Another issue which often works against the patient and particularly against the family is "confidentiality." Under this shield of privacy hospitals can and do refuse to give parents information about their child's condition. Granted, adult patients in general have a right to confidentiality between themselves and their doctors, but the situation of the mentally ill is not the situation of general patients. Many of the adult chronically mentally ill are, in effect, children in their judgments and reactions. Do professionals realize what emotional and psychological hurt they are inflicting on parents when they withhold information? Would a doctor refuse to give information to the parents of a cancer patient?

When parents' rights to be given information about the condition of their mentally ill child are denied because of so-called patients' rights, the line between being reasonable and being unreasonable has been crossed.

During the time Danny was committed to a Boston hospital for six months, I was never told how he was doing. I was in complete darkness about his prognosis, whether positive or negative. Each time I questioned the social worker assigned to his case, which was almost daily, the answer would be, "Danny would not give us permission today to tell you how he was doing."

This was the reply I received for the first month or so. Then one day, moved by pity because of the state of anxiety I was in, she replied to my inquiry, "Danny would not give us permission today to tell you how he was doing but the patients on the ward are doing well today."

I grasped at her coded message with much relief. But after hearing that same coded message and only that for the remainder of his commitment, it became quite evident to me that the system was as ill as my son and needed much help.

In most state hospitals voluntary patients have the right to write "a three-day letter" requesting discharge in three days from the date of the letter. Unless the staff can convince the patient he or she would be better off staying in the hospital, discharge must be granted.

Such discharges are seldom in the best interests of the patient. The letter is usually written in anger or frustration. The patient wants out because he or she is dissatisfied with the treatment or surroundings or cannot stand being with the other patients. Since the patients usually do not accept the fact that they are sick, their schizophrenic logic sounds perfectly sensible to them as they muster reasons as to why they no longer need hospitalization. But the fact is that they are sick, and chronic patients who leave a hospital under the three-day letter invariably seek readmittance in a very short time.

Sometimes it seems that the three-day letter is a charade played by administrators, staff, and the politicians who pass the legislation, to give an illusion of freedom—since they should know that inevitably, in almost all cases, the patient will return. On occasion the letter and discharge are used by staff as a means of proving to patients that they are, in fact, sick and unable to cope in the outside world. Sometimes, after devastating experiences, the patients will admit they can't cope, but more often they will not admit it. They simply do not see themselves as sick people. Lora, for instance, went through several such discharges and readmissions before she admitted she needed more help.

And there is another facet of the discharges that must be considered—the suffering of the family.

> *Each time Lora* left the hospital under voluntary discharge, I went through an agony of fear, not knowing what was going to happen to her. Her judgment about people was poor; she accepted as friends men and women she scarcely knew. Because she wanted to help the poor and unfortunate, she would walk through the city distributing dollar bills indiscriminately. Every time my phone rang I was afraid it was the police, telling me they had found her body in an alley, her throat slit by somebody who had stolen her money from her. Only another parent in similar circumstances could understand the relief I felt when she was finally brought back to the hospital each time.

While many of the chronically mentally ill are basically very intelligent, they do not have the ability to control their thoughts or their situations, especially when they are in an acute state. To depend on their judgment is comparable to asking young children whether or not they want to be treated when they are ill. How can we expect the mentally ill to make sensible judgments relative to patients' rights when they don't even have the ability to function in the community on their own?

> *Thomas was not* able to make it on his own outside the hospital for even a few days after having been discharged recently. He was discharged on a three-day letter, left the state, and the following day was asking to be admitted to a hospital. Through a mental health facility, he was admitted to a general hospital where he was allowed to remain for two days. As he had no money left, we were contacted to provide his return transportation. We sent him a prepaid bus ticket which he was unable to use as the bus driver would not admit him on the bus because of his highly agitated condition. Again we were contacted, and we agreed Thomas could return by cab. We would pay for it when he arrived. On his return to Massachusetts, he was pre-screened at a local hospital before he was returned to the state hospital.
> The pre-screening professionals said that Thomas was at great risk in returning with only the cab driver in the taxi with him because of his highly agitated state. The cab driver was also at great risk. I wonder how the out-of-state professionals ever allowed Thomas to leave under those dangerous circumstances.

It becomes clear that, except in a very few cases, patients cannot be discharged from a hospital directly into the community on the premise that they are able to function capably. The great majority of chronically mentally ill patients need very close and constant aftercare. They cannot be "dumped" on the streets. There must be a program for the patients whereby they will have the opportunity to exhibit their functioning capabilities before they are allowed to go off on their own. They need a structured living situation that gives them security at the same time that they are being encouraged to become independent, self-respecting members of society. If the patients do not have sufficient aftercare support, they will invariably fail to adjust to community living.

> *Danny's commitment will* be over soon, and I am so worried. He needs to be recommitted but, according to the present law, it would be difficult to do so because he has improved somewhat. He is progressing slowly but nicely. Putting him out on the streets again will bring him back to "day one." The results of this action are always drastic, and my fear is that this time it could be fatal.
>
> What puzzles me is that I was always under the impression that the sick would be taken care of. But somehow we have deviated from that right that belongs to everyone, and in its place we are inflicting more pain and suffering on the mentally ill, as if their suffering was not already enough.

An increasing number of parents feel there should be a law making it mandatory that mentally ill patients who have a history of being bounced in and out of hospitals be placed in a structured facility for a long enough period of time to definitely prove they can make it on their own. This facility would be attractive and staffed by enough experienced people, offer programs geared to interest the patients, and also help them find jobs. This would entail a large appropriation from the mental health department but families would be so overjoyed to have such a facility they would be glad to help maintain it once it was set up.

The mentally ill for too long a time have been the

"forgotten people." It is high time more money be appropriated for the betterment of the patients. The shelters now being provided are a first step but much, much more has to be done to ensure the help that has so long been denied to the mentally ill.

Chapter 5

Keeping a Life of One's Own

One often sees articles or books about the stresses of modern living and how to cope with them. It has been popular in recent years to compare the stresses of various life situations such as divorce, death in the immediate family, loss of employment, natural disasters, or physical illness. All these are certainly stress-provoking but none more so than living with someone who has a serious mental illness.

It seems impossible in the midst of the day-by-day trauma such a life produces to manage to keep one's own hopes, ambitions, and sense of accomplishment alive. The more difficult such an undertaking may seem, the more important it is to strive to do just that.

Over the years of Lora's illness, 15 long years, I have felt guilt, despair, paranoia and, at times, completely cut off from the "real" world. Finally, I realized that I was not to blame for her mental illness, that despair was one of the emotions I would have to learn to live with, that people were not whispering about my inadequacies as a mother, and that if they were, they spoke out of ignorance, and I must not let their ignorance affect my life.

Fortunately, during all this time I had a full-time job as a newspaper reporter and feature writer on a daily paper, and professionally I was doing well. I also had the gift—I call it a gift under the circumstances—of being able to concentrate wholly on what I was doing while I worked, and since my work was very involving, I did not brood about my daughter when I was on the job. That is, for the most part. But there were occasions when my situation did intrude on my thoughts while I sat at my typewriter or did interviews. Then I knew her condition and mine were in bad shape, and I would make a conscious effort to clear my mind of the intruding thoughts. There was nothing I could do to help her at that time, and the brooding did neither of us any good.

I am a person who truly enjoys life. The despair and depression brought about by my daughter's illness were foreign to my attitudes and thinking. I knew instinctively that I must not lose my individuality if I were to survive—and I couldn't help Lora if I didn't survive. I think that my optimism and my zest for life were attributes my daughter clung to. I think every ill child clings to his or her image of the mother as an anchor in a very confusing world, and the mother must preserve that image by being her own natural self.

There is also the very important fact of preserving your own sanity through activities that make and keep you your own person. In my case, it meant going to the theater which I love, seeing old friends and having conversations that included subjects other than mental illness, making new friends so that my horizons continue to broaden, playing bridge, a game I enjoy, as often as possible. Doing it all without guilt. In fact, because I preserved my integrity as a person, I sensed that my daughter respected me more—even if she couldn't spell out the reasons—and that she looked forward to seeing me.

It's a long, hard road to acceptance and self-consideration and even now I sometimes fall into despair but work and personal pleasures are great allies, and they can make life more than just bearable.

Mothers and fathers who make the effort to cope with the daily disturbances of their children's mental illness will often find an inner strength they did not guess they had. It is a solace that calms the turmoil within, and it can be an inspiration to others in the family.

> *"This reminds me* of you, Mom. Keep it!" said my daughter as she handed me the tag to the tea bag she was about ready to use. The little message on the tag read, "The human spirit is stronger than anything that can happen to it."
>
> I never saw myself quite that way but was pleased that she did. Danny's illness has taken its toll on me, but I guess I'm able to hide more and cope better than I think. Maybe it's because I love to laugh and enjoy seeing and hearing other people laugh. I also keep as busy as I can.
>
> Many are the times when, thinking about Danny's lost life, I find the pain unbearable. That's when I have a good cry, say a prayer and then try to put a positive thought in my mind. After a while the pain eases and I pick myself up and get involved in something. It could be baking a cake, calling up a friend, going out shopping or making fun plans.
>
> Also, being active in the Alliance for the Mentally Ill helps a great deal—not only through the love and support of friends who understand the pain but also in the knowledge that you are helping the mentally ill and their families. This takes away any guilt feelings you may have when enjoying other aspects of life.
>
> I also remind myself that life is not forever anyway so I may as well make the best of it and that maybe, just maybe, there will be a miracle around the corner.

When a family member is mentally ill, his or her enormous needs can absorb all the attention and energies of others in the group. There is a tyranny in the way one person is able to manipulate the behavior of others. The power to control the actions of others must be a very unsettling feeling, especially when that very person feels so little in control of his or her own behavior.

Perhaps the family ties, loves, and loyalties are too strong for a sick person to cope with. This may be the reason the disoriented person often seems more stable and predictable when being cared for by people unrelated to him. A kind attendant sometimes is more able to provide help. He is less likely to fall victim to the manipulations of the disturbed one. There is a distance he is able to maintain that a close relative usually doesn't have. Also, at the end of his shift, the attendant goes home and restores his energies in his own environment.

Nevertheless, it is sometimes necessary to have a mentally disturbed person living in the family circle. It is important to remember that the more one gives in to the behavior and demands of a person suffering schizophrenia, the more it seems to exacerbate the disturbance. It takes energy and determination to proceed with one's own life while a loved one is existing in some private hell of his own. It may seem selfish and cold at times to turn your back on his or her turmoil but those who have lived in this situation often agree it is in everyone's best interest.

Keeping a life of my own just couldn't be done when Jean lived at home. It was like walking on eggshells. We were afraid of doing the slightest thing that might set her off. It might have been the way we held our hands or fingers, the way we would look or something we said. She would think that something was wrong. We couldn't take her anywhere because everything upset her. We couldn't leave her alone because of the fear that something might happen to her.

Then there was my own guilt. Had I done something wrong? Was I to blame for what happened? My whole world was falling apart. However, with a great deal of help from counselors, social workers, and many good friends in the Alliance for the Mentally Ill, my life is a lot better now.

After being in and out of hospitals for the last five years, Jean is living in a community house in our hometown. I go to see her once a week and talk to her every day on the telephone. She seems happy, and this makes me happy. It's a long road but I'm learning to cope with it.

Our life as a family is beginning to take shape again. We are doing the things we have been unable to do for a very long time, such as going out to dinner, having friends visit, going on vacation, or just taking in a movie. It has been hard for us because we are a very close family. We wish our daughter could do more things with us, but that's not possible right now. My life goes on without guilt or blame for Jean's illness. I'm going to stay happy and healthy.

The task of keeping one's own individuality and interests alive while living with someone who is chronically disorganized seems insurmountable. Nevertheless, it is probably the only real way one can help a sick relative. Parents who lose sight of the world around them won't help the one who is ill. The health and well-being of mother and father, brother and sister are more important than ever in order to maintain equilibrium during the difficult days. Small pleasures and indulgences can help restore balance in life.

This past week was so bad. I cried at the littlest thing. I wanted to sleep even more than usual and felt all my projects to be useless. I would have been relieved if my life was suddenly over. The thought of Danny's never-ending problem was overwhelming. He was doing so well for a while, and my hopes seemed to soar. But again the turning point backwards. It came at a time when my own physical and mental output was low, causing me to go backwards with him.

"I must not dwell on this," I thought and called a friend from the Alliance. Her understanding heart and wise advice gave me the spark I needed to recharge myself and put my thinking back in proper perspective. After our talk, I picked myself up and met with a friend for coffee, an appointment I was earlier thinking of cancelling. I was so happy I didn't. We talked, mostly of other matters, had a few laughs and did a little window shopping. It was so good to think about other things.

The past few years since I have been trying to keep a life of my own have been a great help to me. It also seems to give other members of my family the courage we all so desperately need when they see me enjoy other aspects of life. I feel it's also healthier for Danny to see me with a smile rather than a frown. Both are contagious, and you may as well pass on the better one. Our mentally ill children need just as much inspiration as we do, if not more.

Dinner out occasionally, a movie, vacations, and so on give us temporary relief from worry, sadness and despair. They are refreshing like a good night's sleep. Accepting the problem and then learning to live around it seem to be the only answer.

When an illness cannot be explained, when the medical community can provide no real answers, either for cause or cure, it is very human to search for something or someone to blame. Husbands and wives are sometimes drawn into criticism of one another. Who among us has been a perfect parent? It isn't hard to find evidence of shortcomings in one's mate or oneself. Families can be split apart by the tragedy of mental illness. They can also draw closer together and unite, finding greater strength to provide a stable atmosphere for themselves as well as their afflicted relative.

It is a sad thing to realize that having a mentally ill child can destroy a marriage. Coping requires an enormous amount of patience, compassion, and mutual support between husbands and wives. Husbands have walked out on their families because they could no longer face the disruption in their lives. Wives have retreated from responsibility and reality as the heartbreak of dealing with mental illness beats them down.

Experience has shown mothers are apt to be stronger in coping with the ongoing crises of mental illness than fathers. Observed at mutual support group meetings, fathers in general seem less able, less willing to face the fact that their sons or daughters are mentally ill. They blame the erratic actions on character defects, on the mother's "too sympathetic" attitude, on peer influence, on sheer willfulness, on street drugs. They refuse to admit to the possibility of an actual mental problem. They develop mental blocks that become rigid and immovable. Often they withdraw totally from the problem. Sometimes, if the marriage continues, the father will eventually come round to facing the reality of chronic mental illness, and life for the family improves. The change of attitude in the father will also benefit the mentally ill child.

It is a heartwarming thing to see a husband and wife supporting each other from the start, loving their ill child and together working for the best possible conditions. Nobody can know what agonies they may endure privately but to the world they show a determined, loving exterior that gives encouragement to their child and inspiration to other families.

From the start the mother should realize that the illness of their son or daughter is just as hard on her husband as it is on her. He may show less emotion, less pain, but his suffering is no doubt equal to hers.

When the burden seems to "get" to my husband, more tired than usual, eyes saddened by the prospects, I can lift his spirits as he has lifted mine so often with his wonderful sense of humor.

"Look," I say, "we have done the best we know how. We will continue to do everything possible and appropriate. Now give it over. Let tomorrow wait for tomorrow."

My advice to husbands and wives is to maintain your own good health. Keep in touch with family and friends in your town and church and the Alliance. Attend your respective jobs and be ever "on the ready" for the unpredictable.

Although data comparing the rate of violence by the chronic mentally ill with the regular population are conflicting, Steadman, Vanderwyst and Ribner report[5] that patients who have not been arrested before hospitalization do not have a higher rate of arrests for crimes after discharge than the regular population. Some statistics indicate that there are fewer crimes by the mentally ill recorded after discharge than in the regular citizenry.

Even so, society fears the mentally ill because there is little understanding or knowledge about the illness, and where there is ignorance, there is fear. The only way to combat this ignorance and fear is through education. It is important for those living with a schizophrenic to talk to others about it, to help educate and familiarize the public with the facts of the illness. There is little fear felt by those who are most familiar with the problems. Witness the one small female attendant in a state hospital who routinely leads a group of a dozen or more severely disturbed people in their daily programs.

In some cases, circumstances of daily living force the disturbed person too close to the world he fears. He may lash out in his confusion and fright. Those closest to him, his family, are most likely to be the ones in his way and, therefore, the most likely to be hurt. But it is seldom a murderous violence.

I remember once when Danny got up from a chair and rushed over to strike me as I was not careful with my words, and he heard something he didn't like. I ran out of the house, and he turned on his father. To this day I'm sure Danny does not recall this incident, and if he did, he would blame it on the devil and spirits.

The thought of being attacked and physically harmed by another is frightening in itself, but when the attacker is your own flesh and blood, it is additional, unspeakable trauma upon trauma as your whole being sways between love and fear.

If a stranger were to be the attacker, you would automatically try to defend yourself, but when it is the one you love, you only try to run because your love would bind your hands.

The fear of violence makes living with a schizophrenic very difficult, even if it is violence directed only towards things, like smashing objects. You always have to be on guard about what you say or how you look at that person. Then you worry that he may hear or see something through his own disorder and associate it with you. In short time you are worn out, and your own mental health is at stake.

A family's world seems to collapse when one of its members becomes mentally ill. The initial shock and disbelief can render a whole family immobile. Getting beyond this stage is a truly Herculean task. During the early years it is very common to spend much time and energy looking for causes. This can be exacerbated by professionals, who often examine whole families with a fine-tooth comb, all the while assuring the parents that they are in no way to blame. Now there is a double bind situation.

As the years multiply, some families and some individuals within families manage to grow and mature and learn from this tragic experience. They find ways of coping with what had seemed in the beginning an impossible situation. They reach heights of wisdom, tolerance and understanding they had not known before. It is particularly difficult for the family with a sick member who continues to live in their midst. The family is torn between the need to nurture and shelter their sick member and the need to lead a more normal life. How can life go on in a positive and healthy way when the most ordinary situation can be turned upside down in seconds by the disturbed behavior of a mentally ill person? How does a teenager entertain his peers at home when his sick brother or sister can make a mockery of every social occasion? How does an older couple invite friends to their home when they are aware their son or daughter is cowering in fear by the intrusion of outsiders? What happens to small children when a sick parent is too confused to give them proper care?

The uncertainties, the unspoken fears, the topsy-turvy world created in the wake of schizophrenia can lead some families to search out almost any solution to their problem. It is a measure of the desperation felt by some of these families that they have actually moved away from their sick member, deliberately covering their trail to make it impossible for their schizophrenic relative to find them. Such a solution is extreme but it does happen. Thinking about "getting away from it all" is fairly common, but most families remain to face whatever life may bring.

There are positive actions that can be taken to make life more bearable when a family member is mentally ill.

1) Do as much as you can financially and physically to improve the situation but don't feel guilty about all you won't be able to do. If it isn't possible to maintain a degree of peace, dignity and well-being within the family while the schizophrenic or manic-depressive person lives at home,

other arrangements should be made. If it is necessary, don't be embarrassed in seeking public support through available social services such as community clinics and state hospitals. You have every right to ask for information and help from the facilities of your state Department of Mental Health. Tax dollars are meant to support the truly disabled.

2) Strive for good physical health. Both the mentally disturbed one and the other family members will benefit from a proper diet, a regular exercise routine, and a clean, orderly living environment.

3) Watch your stress level. Don't let yourself burn out. Put on the brakes when you feel yourself sliding into an untenable situation, when your nerves start to jump. A game of solitaire, an hour watching an interesting television program, a hot, luxurious bath, meditation, a walk around the block, digging and weeding in the garden—anything that stops or changes the direction of your thoughts can be helpful.

Remember that no life is without stress. Learning how to cope with it is the key to making and keeping a life of your own. Look for what gives you peace of mind and enjoy it: a walk on the beach or in the woods; a movie, a play, a good book, a painting; a conversation with a dear friend; a prayer. The point is to let yourself go, to relax, to let your body and mind renew itself, thus recharging your energy.

4) An effort to maintain social contacts is imperative. If a family member becomes ill with a debilitating physical illness—heart disease or cancer, for instance—neighbors, friends and peripheral family members are often very supportive. If the illness is mental, the family involved usually feels stigmatized. The family unit often withdraws with their sick relative from the community at large. It is

much better if they continue to circulate in as normal a way as possible. Such families are in a unique position to break down the walls of prejudice and fear that surround mental illness. If communication exists between afflicted families and their neighbors, there is often a great deal of compassion and understanding expressed.

5) Seek out one of the many groups recently formed by families of the mentally ill. There is much comfort and knowledge shared by such groups. If a group hasn't been formed in your community, you might start one. (See chapter on networks.)

6) Continue pursuing your own interests. Burying one's hopes and desires in order to placate the demands of a mentally disturbed person will add to the problem, not diminish it.

If you are an artist, continue to draw and paint. If you are a potter, continue to work with clay. If you enjoy woodworking, if you jog, if you are an active club member, continue to do those things that give you pleasure and make your life fulfilling. You will be better able to cope with your problems because, at least to a degree, you will still be your own person. Don't let resentment build up in you because you have given up interests and dreams to meet the demands of your mentally ill family member. It will do neither one of you any good. Be kind to yourself as well as to the patient.

7) Do something for someone else. Our own problems seem less defeating when we are involved in giving support to others.

Chapter 6

Dealing With Professionals

One of the first and most frustrating aspects for the parents of the long-term mentally ill is dealing with professionals, particularly psychiatrists. For centuries doctors have nurtured their god-like image, and when parents first become involved with the world of the mentally ill, they are usually intimidated to the point of speechlessness when they come face to face with a psychiatrist. Who are they to question the wisdom of the all-knowing doctor seated on his pedestal?

Looking back on early experiences, parents can see how far they have come in dealing with the unreal world of mental illness and the professional caretakers.

I found it very hard to deal with professionals during the early years of Danny's illness. Perhaps it was due to my own personality, being at times shy, awkward and afraid of saying the wrong thing.

One particular instance I remember vividly. My son was committed to a Boston hospital for six months. After six months he was not at all better and in many ways worse. The hospital would not consider Danny for re-commitment because he refused medication.

At a family meeting the day before he was to be discharged, my body and mind went numb as I listened to the doctor. I couldn't believe my ears. He said we had two choices. Danny could either come home or we could get him a room somewhere. Both considerations were unthinkable. I have an illness that is debilitating so I couldn't give Danny proper care. It was also clear he needed more professional treatment.

I could barely speak but managed to mumble, "How can you do this?"

The doctor sat there, not moving an inch. He looked like a statue placed there by some strange god and without any emotion replied to me sternly, "Do you know how many hundreds are walking the streets of Boston with no place to go?"

Being unaware of what was truly going on in the world around me, this horrible information was news to me and placed me not only in a greater state of shock but also made me feel guilty that I was considering my son to be better than any other human being. I bowed my head and was silent.

If this situation were to happen to me today, I would retort. "Then it's high time we do something about it, with the doctors at the helm, for it is in your hands with the oath you have taken to care for the ill and to lead the way."

The frustrations that arise when a family member is ill and seeing a psychiatrist are difficult to deal with. The doctor must keep everything his patient tells him in confidence if they are to have any kind of trusting relationship. Nevertheless, the family needs to know what is going on and to have input, too. This is especially important if the mentally ill person lives at home.

Some doctors face this problem by asking their patient's permission to have family members attend an occasional session, always with the patient present. This does help somewhat. Other doctors prefer to work with a psychologist who will meet with the family, acting as an intermediary between the psychiatrist and the family. This method can be cumbersome and expensive and doesn't really face the issue of complete confidentiality.

Parents meeting with professionals can make it a positive action. If it accomplishes nothing else, it at least gives parents an opportunity to express their feelings and concerns. More and more hospitals, both private and state-operated, are scheduling these meetings as a means of providing more relevant treatment. All parental suggestions are not automatically accepted but they can be an opening wedge in the long battle toward individual treatment.

> *Family meetings with* professionals were always difficult for me. However, I always attended hoping David would gain something from them. I had long since given up expecting any benefit for myself that would compensate for the dredging up of old guilt feelings, justified or not, in the retelling of my son's medical history or the annoyance of having to detail his early years: When did he start to walk? When was he toilet trained? How was his relationship with his father? "Ah, hmmmm," drifts a murmur from the next chair. When did he start dating? How were his studies? And on and on for the umpteenth time, all of which has been documented by typewriter, photocopy, mimeograph, and probably microfilm many times before.

It takes years of bitter experience for parents to realize that psychiatrists do not have the answers, that in a practical sense psychiatrists know little more than the parents themselves about day-to-day treatment of schizophrenia, that in fact a parent's knowledge about his or her child can be of enormous help in setting up a program for the patient.

Slowly some psychiatrists, psychologists, and social workers are recognizing these truths and admitting them. And as they work more closely with parents, horizons are broadened, new treatment approaches are tested and hope, a spindly plant at best, puts out tentative roots.

There is a growing trend for family members and professionals to meet together at seminars and confer- ences where families can express their feelings and con- cerns, working toward mutual understanding and trust. It is an educational process for the professionals as well as the families, making clear the benefits of working together.

The ability of parents to grow in understanding and self-confidence has been evident in seminars held in Mas- sachusetts. They have learned to confront the profession- als calmly and rationally, expressing their feelings with candor. The following piece was written by David's mother, who, with her husband, participated in a panel discussion at an area workshop. Here it is as she presented it.

"A *strained relationship* between parents and profession- als has developed over a long period of time and is rooted, I believe, in the neo-Freudian school of therapy which maintains children's mental and emotional disorders are directly related to parental rearing. Parents were, therefore, found guilty and excluded, even isolated, from treatment of their children by most professionals. Indeed, as little information as possible regarding their loved one's condi- tion and treatment was made available to parents. To cite one example, although the name of the medications pre- scribed for my son David might be given upon request, no explanation of its purpose was readily offered, and because I wasn't aware there would be side effects and, therefore, did not press for this information, I did not learn of the possible side effects until they became so noticeable in David's behavior as to be considered irreversible.

"Added to the sense of guilt which is imposed on parents is a frustration from growing awareness that in many cases there is little hope for recovery. Family problems increase, and the psychiatrist seems to become more and more inaccessible, protected from anxious parents by his secretary, by the social worker who intercepts requests for information or the staff member of the clinic who makes excuses for the absence of the doctor.

"Parents need to hear the truth from professionals so that a relationship of trust can be established and so they can act as an informed advocate for their loved one who in many cases is helpless.

"I have observed that the afflicted with whom I am acquainted send out conflicting signals, which is a symptom of the disease, but it is evident that they love their parents, are not a threat to society, and are not criminals. These are not children of unloving parents; these are not children of homes where they are not wanted. We grieve that our children cannot live with us, but we have learned that they do not prosper in our homes.

"So we ask professionals to listen to a different tune, one which embraces and accepts parents and looks to other possible causes of the disease than environment."

When the conference was over, I was approached by a member of the audience who thanked me and said, "It must have been hard for you to speak up. That took a lot of courage." I didn't tell her she was wrong on both counts. It wasn't hard. It was easy. I was happy to have the opportunity to express my concerns and hope for improvement in parent-professional relationships. It didn't take courage. We parents are ready and willing to take up any task that will give us the answers we are looking for.

There are very positive steps and positive attitudes that parents can take to improve their situation. Choosing a doctor / psychiatrist is the first and probably the most important step.

An acute psychotic break is most often apt to be the catalyst for seeking professional help. It is almost impossible in such chaotic conditions to make any sort of intelligent inquiry into professional services available. Luck plays a big part in the quality of help one finds. However, there are a few points that can help in choosing a doctor if the search is not too hurried or even if it is, you can check the points when the dust settles.

1) Be wary of any doctor who offers a cure. To date, no cure has been found for long-term mental illness.

2) Human relationships are very personal. You should instinctively like and trust the doctor you choose. If you have misgivings, don't waste valuable time. Ask for another reference.

3) Choose a doctor who does his best to make it easy for you to reach him. Mental illness will not keep office hours. Help is often needed on long holiday weekends or in the middle of the night.

4) Don't be embarrassed about discussing finances. Be sure the cost of therapy is made clear and that the methods of finding financial help are explained to you.

5) Family visits to a psychiatrist, psychologist, therapist, or any kind of counselor can be helpful and enlightening or totally frustrating. Before you go, spend an hour or so thinking about the things you want to talk about. In the quiet of your own home it is easier to focus on all the troubled areas you want to bring up.

6) Make a brief outline of the topics you want to discuss with your counselor. Bring it with you and refer to it from time to time. It will help keep the conversation on the things that will be of most help to you. The 50-minute psychiatric hour passes very quickly. The most skilled professional cannot be expected to read your mind. It is

up to you, the consumer, to milk the time for all it's worth.

7) Don't let yourself be intimidated by professionals. Remember that they are human beings just like you despite their professional trappings. Don't be afraid to ask questions or make suggestions. After all, in certain aspects nobody knows the patient better than the parents.

8) It is important to remember you have a right to understand the explanations you are given. If the terms the doctor uses are too technical, request a rephrasing in simpler words. If you know you will not be able to remember all that he is telling you, ask him to write down the key or important points.

9) As a parent you should be informed about the nature of the treatment proposal. If there are alternatives to the treatment, you should be told about them. The cost of treatment and methods for payment should be clarified. If there are risks, they should be explained.

10) Be honest with the professionals you talk to. It is unproductive to withhold your viewpoint. To be afraid of sharing the truth about how you feel is a mistake, hurting both the patient and the therapist. To develop a good positive relationship with the therapist, parents must speak the truth as they see it at that moment.

11) Look for the best in the professional you are working with and tell him what his qualities are that you appreciate and are thankful for. Use that as the base for telling him / her what troubles you. If a therapist won't talk to you, ask for a different therapist.

12) Don't put a professional on the defensive. Be as tactful and pleasant as possible. Remember that professionals are essentially teachers. They have been trained in this, and you should encourage them to tell you what they know. At the same time realize that you have something to teach them and insist that they allow you to share your

wisdom with them though this is sometimes difficult to achieve.

13) Insist, too, that you be treated with respect. Be prepared for occasions when you will need to be assertive—not aggressive, not unpleasant, and not passive—but holding your own. Assertive is not a dirty word. It simply means knowing what your bottom lines are and not being afraid to ask and negotiate for what you want. Occasionally it may be necessary to go over the head of the professional you are working with. He or she has a superior, just like everybody else, and is accountable.

14) Ask professionals how they think you can be most helpful to the patient. You don't have to agree or accept their advice but you may learn something that can improve the situation. Find out when the professionals expect to see positive results from this action; then you can both measure its effectiveness. If you try the professionals' suggestions in good faith, in the future they may be more open to your suggestions.

15) Remember that nobody has "*the* answer" to mental illness. The professionals need you as much as you need them—even if they don't know it. Working with them won't come easy. You will have to give as much, maybe more, than you get. You will be torn emotionally. You will be frustrated, hurt, angry—but occasionally there will be times of pleasure and satisfaction when you know there has been a positive response, with some measurable results.

16) Ask yourself: "Am I willing to grow and change through this experience? Am I willing to be uncomfortable and vulnerable in the process of learning to deal with a challenging situation?" If your answers are negative, don't expect the professional to change and grow either. There must be mutual interaction for mutual benefit.

All these suggestions for positive attitudes and actions

are easily stated. Making them a reality will be a longer process. In the meantime, as we work toward the ideal, we continue to learn from the shared experiences of parents, any one of whom may be one step ahead of us.

Chapter 7

Beyond Talk Therapy and Pills

It is a basic fact that nobody expects to find one cure that will magically eliminate mental illness. Schizophrenia, for instance, is an umbrella term that embraces a variety of illnesses of the mind. Each patient must be treated individually. Megavitamins may help one patient and not another. But the profession must come to realize that if megavitamins, as one example, can help only one out of every 500 patients, that would, in fact, be helping thousands. Other treatments, other programs may help thousands more. Psychiatrists, most of them still hidebound by the talk-therapy, medication theory, must recognize and act upon the fact that there are indeed many more ways of treating schizophrenia. And when psychiatrists turn their backs on new theories because, they say, these new theories have not been scientifically proven, parents of schizophrenics have a right to ask: By what scientific method has talk therapy been proven effective? The great majority of parents of the long-term mentally ill see their children going in and out of hospitals, finding it impossible to cope in the outside world, and they know that talk therapy has failed.

One day when I went to see a consulting psychiatrist, I had no reason to believe any new treatment for my son David would be forthcoming, nor would there be any change in the diagnosis. But I rationalized that there was nothing to lose in going, and perhaps there were some gains to make. At least David would have an opportunity to meet the consultant, and if there were some rapport between them, he might seek his aid sometime in the future—a thin thread of hope to build on.

As I drove to the meeting, I prepared myself, as I always did, with prayer, a prayer that God's love and wisdom would be present in our minds and hearts. I had prepared some questions, starting with a request that arrangements be made for David to see a dentist.

I inquired also about recent scientific developments that might have surfaced since the advent of EEGs and CAT scans. I had heard of a three-dimensional scan known to me as the PET scan which might reveal the cause of schizophrenic symptoms and lead to better medications. Currently used medications can cause tardive dyskinesia and its cousin dystonia, resulting in involuntary muscle dysfunction; these side effects can be very debilitating and painful for some patients, often manifesting themselves in involuntary turning of the neck and head or twisting of the body. Although these contortions have been thought to be irreversible in cases of long endurance, this is not the current prognosis for all patients.

According to this psychiatrist, diagnosis and research for many illnesses are greatly enhanced by the use of PET scans, CAT scans and nuclear magnetic resonance, which can, for example, detect tumors and scars not otherwise visible. However, a good correlation has not been made between what can be seen and schizophrenic symptoms, and he did not believe scans were yet useful in diagnosis of patients with this disease.

The subject of nutrition had not been addressed, and I asked if the doctor would consider a comprehensive vitamin program and put more emphasis on good nutrition. I know that treatment with vitamins is controversial but I was satis-

fied that again I had an opportunity to stress the importance of an individualized nutrition plan for David. On a
separate consultation, a popular multivitamin had been prescribed but I was hoping for a more personal appraisal of
David's supplement needs.

Nutrition and vitamin therapy opens a whole world of
new possibilities in the treatment of long-term mental illness. There are many other possibilities, ranging from the
importance of pleasant, supportive environments to the
elimination or decreasing use of antipsychotic drugs to the
theory of viral infection. In between are new attitudes in
the mental health profession growing out of research that
opens new doors in the understanding of mental illness. It
is an encouraging sign that some changes are occurring
among professionals.

Several years ago, after Lora had been in the state hospital for about three years, she had reached a condition where
she could function no better than a vegetable. At times she
was catatonic. She had regressed to 14 years of age. The
staff didn't know what to do for her. When I suggested to
the head psychiatrist that they try orthomolecular treatment—highly controlled nutrition and megavitamins—the
doctor literally laughed at me. "We would never consider
that," she said.

After many years of ups and downs, my daughter was
again in the same hospital and again obviously needed a
different kind of treatment. I knew it was too much to expect
the hospital to provide a nutritious, healthful diet, but I asked
the new psychiatrist in charge if he would prescribe vitamins if I bought them and brought them to the dispensing
nurse. He said, yes, he would. It was the first ray of hope I
felt. And the vitamins did help Lora. She very soon began
to think more clearly.

A short time later the same psychiatrist, at the request

of his staff and with the support of members of the local Alliance for the Mentally Ill, ordered that only decaffeinated coffee be served in the hospital. He and is staff had clearly observed that caffeine hyper-activated the patients, making them difficult to control.

These two accomplishments, regarding vitamins and decaffeinated coffee, have given me hope that progress is possible.

There are several alternative treatments parents can consider, and their number is growing. Today it is generally accepted that schizophrenia and other chronic mental illnesses are biochemical and / or genetic disorders. They are diseases just as diabetes, multiple sclerosis, arthritis and other ailments are diseases, and they need to be treated medically. Traditional psychotherapy as the only treatment for schizophrenia is increasingly regarded as inadequate and possibly negligent. In fact, psychoanalysis and other insight-oriented psychotherapies have little demonstrated value in this illness.

Though funding for research on mental illness is totally inadequate, some new diagnostic approaches and theories are surfacing. Some doctors think there may be a viral basis for mental illness, and they are pushing for more research in this area. From research it is now known that the brain of a schizophrenic differs from that of a normal person and, consequently, reacts differently. Research in this field may yield some definitive answers on the cause and control of such chronic mental illness.

Over the years medication has improved. Some drugs have been discarded, others introduced. And as an example of outstanding change in attitude and method, consider the use of shock therapy.

In 1938 electroshock treatment was introduced as an

improvement on insulin shock therapy which helped some chronic patients. Electrodes were attached to the patient's head and controllable electric currents were passed through his brain. The patient lost consciousness. The electric current produced a convulsion, and the patient awakened shortly after. Sometimes, as an aftereffect, his memory was clouded but often, particularly in seriously depressed patients, his mental state was much improved. Despite the fact that no one knew how shock therapy worked, its success rate made it a popular form of treatment

The introduction of psychotropic medications in 1952 and the hope they promised made shock treatment seem too dangerous and traumatic. Its use was sharply curtailed. But drug therapy produced its own problems. A certain number of patients didn't respond to the medication. Others suffered debilitating side effects. Today many respected psychiatrists are again advocating shock treatment for some of their patients.

New methods of administering ECT are safer and more comfortable though some memory loss continues to be a side effect. Even though after 50 years little is known about why shock treatment sometimes works, its percentage of success with self-abusive and deeply despondent persons makes it a viable alternative. It is another instance of broadening the range of treatment.

The subject of orthomolecular treatment must be raised even though the great majority of professionals react to it with a scorn that reaches almost manic proportions. Nevertheless, there are thousands of former schizophrenic patients in this country who are residing in their communities, working at jobs and living good lives because of orthomolecular therapy.

The treatment, discovered by two respected Canadian doctors, was given the name "orthomolecular," which was coined by Dr. Linus Pauling, Nobel prize winner in chemistry. "Ortho" means "correct." "Orthomolecular" means "correct molecules." Treatment includes vitamins, minerals and a high protein diet rich in selected fruits and vegetables. It is based on the premise that schizophrenia and some other disorders, including alcoholism, are caused by a biochemical dysfunction or deficiency that affects the function of the brain. Correcting biochemical imbalances provides the brain cells with the proper molecular environment so that they can function normally. Orthomolecular psychiatry holds that the delicately balanced chemistry of the nervous system cannot perform its complex functions unless that balance is biochemically correct.

A growing number of psychiatrists are turning to orthomolecular therapy or some form of it. The Academy of Orthomolecular Psychiatry, founded in 1971, has more than 200 members, each an accredited physician. They have treated more than 50,000 patients. Cures, or marked improvement, have been observed in up to 85 percent of the patients under orthomolecular treatment, according to their statistics. Educational information, support for orthomolecular-treated patients in the community and support for families are available through local chapters of the nationally organized Huxley Institute of Biosocial Research.

> *Orthomolecular treatment is* the closest thing to a miracle that I have seen. My daughter Lora had been in and out of hospitals and psychiatrists' offices for more than six years, her condition deteriorating over the years. She was considered a classic schizophrenic. The last straw was when the head psychiatrist in the state hospital said he didn't know what to do for her and planned to experiment. Experiment! The word conjured up all kinds of horrible Frankenstein possibilities. Lora had gone through a catatonic state. She

was little more than a vegetable. What more would they do to her? I didn't want to find out.

I had been searching desperately for other kinds of treatment. In the nick of time I learned about orthomolecular therapy and found that it was available in New Hampshire. I took Lora out of the state hospital where she was a voluntary patient and drove north with her to the Lakes Regional General Hospital in Laconia where she was under the care of the late Dr. Nathan Brody. In three weeks this young woman was cured beyond any point that psychiatric talk therapy had even aimed for in five years. In fact, without any therapy at all, simply as another patient in a general hospital being treated by a general practitioner, Lora returned to the real world through proper nutrition and megavitamins.

In less than a month after I had taken her out of the state hospital, Lora went into Boston, rented an apartment, hired a practice hall, had a telephone installed, ran an ad for students in a Boston newspaper and started a dance school. I couldn't believe it as I saw it happening. Lora was herself again.

But there was still a bitter experience ahead. I didn't realize at the time that when she came back to Boston, Lora should have had strong back-up support. She should have lived in a supportive system situation where trained personnel would have seen to it that she stayed with her diet and vitamins. As it was, Lora was on her own. And she felt so good she thought she didn't need the vitamins and slowly slipped back into bad eating habits—junk food, doughnuts, caffeine, sugar. She kept going for a while on the original momentum, continuing her school for several months, but the bad food and the chemical imbalance took their toll. And then she was back in the state hospital.

She has never wholeheartedly gone back to the orthomolecular regime, either because of apathy or skepticism. Occasionally she makes a stab at drinking decaffeinated coffee and taking vitamins. I realize now that she was never properly motivated to accept and live by orthomolecular treatment. Three weeks wasn't enough time to psychologically cast out the Freudian influence that, I feel, victimized her. It was much easier and more ego-satisfying to lie on a couch and talk than to follow the discipline of good nutrition. I still firmly believe that if Lora had had the supportive system she needed—and which still does not exist in Massachusetts—she would never have gone back to the hospital.

Though support for patients undergoing new and different kinds of therapy is still rare, there are some programs in this country that do have strong supportive situations. Before becoming involved with programs outside the established norm, families should thoroughly look into the program itself and its post-program follow-up.

The following report was made by the mother and father of a young woman who benefitted from an innovative, supportive program.

The Coral Ridge Hospital in Ft. Lauderdale, Florida, follows the nutrition-megavitamin theory. Our daughter, Erika, likes it better than any hospital she has been in so far.

For eight months she was at the Austin Riggs Hospital in Stockbridge, Massachusetts, where all drugs (medication) were removed, and psychoanalysis was the only tool. It didn't work for her. Then she spent four years and two months at McLean Hospital in Belmont, Massachusetts, where drugs and psychoanalysis were the tools. It worked partially.

At Coral Ridge the treatment includes good nutrition, medication, megavitamins and some psychoanalysis, which seems to be a more rounded therapy.

It is a shame that instead of working together, hospitals go their own way with little or no exchange of ideas and cooperation. Each hospital appears to have one thought, one policy, one approach, and nobody can change or add to it. We feel fortunate that we found Coral Ridge Hospital.

After five weeks at Coral Ridge, vitamins and classes on nutrition have helped Erika greatly. She is looking forward to getting a job. After years of restraints and long periods of isolation, she is now a new person.

Her classes include learning all science knows about mental illness and how good nutrition can help offset the results of mental illness. The staff also gives all the tests needed to pinpoint each person's degree of mental illness. Then they set up a diet for each patient to help the body fight the disease. Each day Erika has three balanced meals plus three small portions of megavitamins and protein along with five hours of classes, two hours of recreation and two hours of free time.

The main problem in foods for an imbalanced brain is sugar, Coral Ridge Hospital teaches. So along with the teaching process, all ways to enjoy foods free of sugar are also taught. They even learn to make sugar-free ice cream.

Nutrition, megavitamins, antipsychotic drugs and psychoanalysis—in that order—seem to be the key to a useful, happy life for today's people disable by mental illness.

Where can parents find treatment other than the conventional psychotherapy and medication? Though facilities that offer alternatives are increasing, their number is still depressingly small. Those that are available are usually privately operated and expensive unless the family has insurance that will cover the costs, or partially cover them.

However, it is important to know about them because their programs can be a goal and inspiration to parents as they try to make changes in their local and state facilities. Here are a few examples of facilities that have reached out in new directions.

Southeast Biosocial Institute, Ft. Lauderdale, Florida, which operates in conjunction with Coral Ridge Hospital. (Refer back to story about Erika in this chapter.) The emphasis here is on nutrition, megavitamins, physical exercise, education about the illness and its treatment and instilling motivation for a better life. Patients are referred to as students because, the staff feels, they are truly there for educational purposes.

Earth House, East Millstone, New Jersey, near Princeton. Opened in February, 1970, by Rosalind LaRoche, a recovered schizophrenic, psychiatric counselor and colleague of Dr. Carl Pfeiffer, Earth House was the first orthomolecular therapeutic community in the country and is recognized worldwide for its holistic approach, healing the whole person.

The 18th century farm provides a home-like atmosphere where patients are like family members, each having daily household responsibilities. The country setting provides contact with domestic animals and an organic garden. The kitchen is free of refined sugar, caffeine and additives. Attention is given to the individual nutritional needs of each member.

Daily exercise is compulsory. A variety of activities include horseback riding, canoeing, drama, visits to museums, concerts, and sporting events. There are also "adventures" similar to those in standard Outward Bound courses. There is craft work, fine arts, music, creative writing, among other programs. Some members attend area colleges.

Earth House works with families to help them overcome guilt and resist manipulation and has training programs for nurses, doctors and other professionals. The holistic center also does research on mental illness. Recovered schizophrenics with special skills are often employed at Earth House because of the unique understanding they have to give.

Bryce Hospital, Tuscaloosa, Alabama, is a state psychiatric facility under the department of mental health. The adolescent unit and the nova program use a nutrition program as part of treatment.

The adolescent unit was inaugurated in 1975 through the efforts of Mr. and Mrs. Glenn Ireland II. At the time, Mrs. Ireland was on the hospital's human rights committee. Mr. Ireland later became commissioner of mental health in Alabama and provided support for development of the nova program, opened in 1982 for young adult chronic schizophrenics.

Opposition to the program has been slight, according to Dr. Cynthia Bisbee, director of the nova unit and of patient education. The staff physicians, other than Dr. Humphry Osmond, who pioneered nutrition-vitamin therapy for schizophrenia, are not enthusiastic but offer no real resistance to the program, Dr. Bisbee said.

At Bryce Hospital studies have shown that schizophrenic patients with bizarre behavior and hyperactivity become much better following a period of time in the nova unit. Nova patients are involved in both the nutrition-vitamin program and a variety of psychosocial treatments. "Schizophrenia is an illness which requires that we come at it from all directions," Dr. Bisbee stated. She said it is her personal opinion that psychosocial treatments, which affect primarily the patients' behavior, and the medication and nutritional program, which affects the internal mental condition, are both necessary for affecting schizophrenic behavior.

With regard to cost, Dr. Osmond has stated that the diet is actually 20 percent less expensive than the "regular" diet, which has more sugar and other refined carbohydrates and processed foods. There is additional expense in supplying such healthful mid-morning and mid-afternoon snacks as peanuts, fruits, juices, and raisins instead of sugary drinks. Popcorn, it was noted, is a good snack that is nutritious and also low-cost. If the dietary program were provided for the entire hospital, it would cost even less because meals would not be considered special and made separately for comparatively few patients.

Napa State Hospital, Imola, California, has had a nutrition-vitamin unit since the mid-1970s, and for more than five years has had the financial support of the California legislature.

Dr. William Bewley, former director of the program, said orthomolecular treatment arouses sharp controversy in the medical community but he believes "we are on the right track." Napa State Hospital has 48 beds in this special unit for the chronically mentally ill. Patients enter the program by choice and must be able to give informed consent. The average patient is in the program for about a year before being released into the community, Dr. Bewley said.

The approach at Napa State is holistic. "We look at the problem like the old family doctor," Dr. Bewley explained. "We assume that the patient is sick, and we look for all possible causes. This does not negate the sociological or psychological approaches but adds to them."

Exercise is an important part of the program. Dr. Bewley said it improves the general tone of the body, gets rid of stagnation and is a welcome change in the patients' lives. "They all report they feel better after they've been jogging or swimming rather than sitting around watching television." Dr. Bewley said.

The program tries to reduce the patients' intake of coffee and cigarettes, and the diet avoids certain foods, flavorings, coloring and chemicals that are known to affect the function of the brain. At Napa the diet is a basic, nutritious hospital diet, with fruit substituted for refined sugars. It includes more vegetables and whole grain cereals and fewer fatty meats. Vitamins are given in megadoses, and the hospital filters the air in an effort to remove allergic factors in the environment which affect the biochemistry of the body and the brain. Since the inception of the program, other medications have been reduced, and few barbituates or sleeping drugs are used.

Each patient is given a series of tests so that individual programs can be set up. The results are proving more than satisfying. "The patients in the program are alert, more in contact," Dr. Bewley said. He added that visitors say the patients look active and bright-eyed. The zombie look is gone.

These are only a few of the programs that exist outside the sacrosanct purviews of the establishment. They are growing in number but families will, generally, have to root them out themselves because the majority of professionals still will not admit they may be helpful.

What can families of the chronically mentally ill do to influence psychiatrists and other mental health professionals toward a more open approach to treatment? How can families get therapists bound to conventional treatments to try more unconventional methods that have, in many cases, proved effective?

There is no easy answer. The first response professionals usually give when asked to try something other than psychotherapy and medication is, "It hasn't been proven effective scientifically." That is not an acceptable answer. Psychotherapy has not been scientifically proven effective either. But to change that unacceptable response parents are going to have to educate themselves, do their own research on alternative treatments and whittle away constantly at the current attitudes of the majority of professionals. Parents will also have to become something of psychologists themselves to understand the professionals they must deal with.

First, parents must remember that professionals tend

to be trained in a specific approach, or approaches, with which they are comfortable. Being human, they are not anxious to change their comfortable ways. Change will be brought about through education and persistence. And the family members must be the persistent educators.

It is also important for families to realize that most professionals are working under bureaucratic and policy restraints. They cannot always do what they want to do, particularly in state institutions, because of state regulations. Families would do well to familiarize themselves with the system and how it works in their areas in order to change it. And it is important to remember that change is often a frightening thing for people, whether family members, patients, or professionals. Understanding is necessary on all sides.

In the meantime, families and patients suffer pain and indignities that should not be tolerated in a civilized world. Parents and relatives work now for basic improvements while they carry in their hearts hope and a vision for a better future.

If an ideal world existed for the mentally ill where money did not dictate treatment or lack of treatment, I could envision a far brighter future for Lora and other unfortunate people affected by schizophrenia. Prejudices against mentally ill people would no longer exist. Society would feel only compassion for the afflicted, and resources for research and care would be generous.

In this utopian society, great care would be used in diagnosing a person's illness. Physical and psychological testing would be extensive. Most malingerers would be weeded out in this process and only those unfortunate people who truly suffer the ravages of this most terrible of diseases would be the recipients of the following care.

Each patient would have his own counselor. The counselor would be highly trained and chosen for his/her compatability with the patient. He would serve as a mentor, a companion, a teacher, a therapist, and a friend.

Medication would be used very sparingly and only after careful evaluation of the patient's needs. Dosage would be constantly reevaluated. Diet and living habits would be monitored as closely as though the patient were recovering from a physical illness. This living arrangement would continue for as long as the patient needed it. It might be for only a few weeks but sometimes the need might continue for months or years, occasionally for a lifetime.

Incentives would be offered to employers willing to hire a mentally ill person. Work would be found befitting the capabilities of each individual. The counselor would be permitted to accompany his charge to the workplace until the patient felt secure enough to be on his own.

The persons accepted for all this care would lose their right to refuse the treatment tailored to their needs. The government would need to guard against abuses very stringently.

If attitudes about mental illness could be so drastically changed, perhaps those who were sick would be more willing to acknowledge their problems and seek help. It is understandable that people are reluctant to admit a mental problem when the mentally ill are faced with scorn and ridicule.

I believe that if the best care were given, even within the bounds of the facts already known, far fewer people would become as sick as they are allowed to be now. Many lives, now wasted, would be salvaged. In the long run the expense to the state would be less because fewer people would need lifetime care.

Utopia indeed. But many ideals have been achieved throughout history, and if the families of the long-term mentally ill appear to be reaching for seemingly unattainable heights, they are at least improving the situation with each step upward.

Chapter 8

Smiling Through the Tears

For families trying to cope with mental illness, the balm of humor, the pleasure of seeing something funny in a situation, the quick lifting of spirits that come from a hearty laugh—or even an ironic smile—these delights of a normal life seem gone forever. But no life should be bereft of humor, and as families come to terms with the illness of a loved one, they often begin to see how funny, ludicrous or absurd a situation is. They may not see it immediately but looking back they may laugh or chuckle over an incident. And that laughter is of great therapeutic value.

We had put in another long day with our son Danny, one of many, and our nerves were worn thin. Sleep was welcome. Suddenly about three o'clock in the morning he woke us all up shouting for us to get him a cab. He had to leave, it was urgent. We all got out of bed and tried to reason with him but as usual nothing made sense and why we even bothered I don't know. He couldn't tell us where he had to go, just that he had to go. I began to rush around in confusion, just like him. Phone books were everywhere as we called one cab after another, trying to find one that operated at that hour. Finally it dawned on me that I would have to give the taxi company a destination, and since I didn't know what it was, I told Danny he would have to talk to them. After about half an hour, with everyone in the family screaming at each other, we located a cab that was running. It had become a state of emergency, and I didn't even know what the emergency was.

While we waited for the cab to arrive, I took my son aside because he would need money for this mystery ride. I wondered how much to give him. My mind rushed on and on. Would he go to California or Arizona again? I had only one hundred dollars in cash on hand and put it in his pocket. I may as well have put the money in the pocket of a two-year-old. As I watched Danny leave in the cab, I wondered how the conversation with the cab driver would go.

I collapsed into bed. I was worried but at the same time it was good to have him out of the house for a while. I went into a deep sleep. The next morning, about mid-morning, I received a call. Danny had gone to his grandmother's house, a half-hour's drive away. Three hours later he was back home.

The tragedy of mental illess can be so overwhelming that sometimes it must be treated with humor in order for the family to survive—be it mother, father, sister, brother or other relatives.

"Do you think things will get better? Do you think things will get better?" It seemed that was all I could ever say. Danny was not improving and, not being able to find any reason, answers or hope, I could say nothing else.

I would call my father, "Papa! Do you think things will get better?" My father would answer, "Liliana, the main thing is to never give up hope and try to put everything out of your mind." It would comfort me for a while, and then I would call a friend. "Do you think things will get better?" She would answer the best she could. When my social worker would visit, I would ask her, and she would try to make me laugh, to ease the pain. "I didn't look at my crystal ball today," she would say. But still I wanted a solid answer.

One day I arrived at my daughter's house, which was on a busy main street. I felt like I weighed a thousand pounds as I dragged one foot after the other. As she came to the door my lips quivered so I was unable to say, "Do you think things will get better?" I just cried, "Oh, Nina!" and she replied, "Oh, Mom!" I quickly turned to face the traffic, and with my arms waving in desperation I cried out, "Does anybody out there know if things are going to get better?"

I looked so funny and sounded so Italian we both roared with laughter.

It is a step toward improved mental health for a distraught mother when she can look back on a frantic situation and shake her head in wonder, chuckling at her near-hysterical reaction to a particular incident.

Every day the telephone would ring about the same time. "Mother, I can't eat the food. It's terrible. I think they are putting poison in it."

Jean, my daughter, was in a psychiatric unit in our local hospital for the first time. I was sure the food wasn't poisoned but it must be terrible if she was unable to eat it. After I hung up I began to think about how alone she must feel, even abandoned, and afraid. She did look a little thinner. She had been away from home for three days. I better make her some dinner, I thought. After all, she was ill, wasn't she?

I arrived at the hospital at five o'clock with my baked stuffed pork chop, mashed potatoes, butternut squash, and, of course, her favorite chocolate cake.

This went on for days. Back and forth I'd go until at last she looked at me and her dinner sternly and said, "I don't want it."

Who was most ill, she or I?" Would I do it again? Not on your life.

Moments of panic are not unusual in family members as they go through the situations of mental illness with their loved ones. Sometimes it seems as though the illness itself rubs off on them, affecting their judgment, their reactions, their emotions. Situations that they could handle rationally if they were not so emotionally involved become threatening. It is fortunate for their own sanity that family members can later look back on such incidents and see the absurdity of their reactions.

During the early years of Danny's periodic hospitalizations walking through the ward would frighten me. Today I still feel great sadness but am more at ease since I have come to know most of the patients. But back in the early years my son was very psychotic and unable to communicate as he lay in his bed staring straight ahead. He had even given himself a different name when the police picked him up, and it was weeks before we knew he had been admitted to the hospital, due to the change in staff, until finally one person recognized him and got in touch with us. During this particular visit back then I had told my friend who was waiting for me downstairs in the lobby I would probably be about an hour, but seeing Danny in the state he was in was too much for me. After about 15 minutes I decided to go home and either cry, sleep, or pray, the only variety then in my life.

Leaving the room, I thought someone would come over to lead me out. Since this was not the case, I began to look for someone. I was not familiar with the office location of the staff or the routine. On this ward the middle doors were locked as well as the one leading to the stairs. My eyes searched each person to see if I could distinguish who was a staff member. When I thought I had found someone, I tapped him or her on the shoulder and asked to be let out. Each would turn and smile strangely at me. Some patients came over to touch me and smile. It frightened me as I thought of the movie "Snake Pit," and the thought of my beautiful son being here was a nightmare. I wandered around in circles for about 10 minutes. Just as I was beginning to feel clammy, I heard a key turn and the middle door opened. I spun around and saw two male workers bringing in a bed. Foolishly I began to run, and I hollered, "Hold that door!" They quickly pushed the bed in and slammed the door shut. I froze as I realized they thought I was a patient.

Act normal, I told myself, and pulled the strap of my bag over my shoulder, thinking I would look more poised. I only looked worse. "Could you let me out?" I asked in an excited voice. "I can't find anyone. I was visiting my son." They smiled and said, "We'll see." "Oh," I babbled nervously, "I'm so happy you're careful. Now I feel more secure about my son being here." And yak, yak, yak. They left me, and I thought my silly mouth must have convinced them I was a patient, and they would not even bother to check me out. I tried to calm myself, telling myself it would only be a matter of time before my friend in the lobby would inquire after me. The workers soon reappeared, and they did lead me out. "Scary wasn't it?" one of the men asked. "A little," I replied, my face flushed.

As I composed myself to meet my friend, I thought of how amazed I used to be that I was still sane after all the experiences in my life. But at that point I was beginning to wonder again about my sanity. Today, I look back on that "locked in" incident and laugh at my foolish panic.

It is often impossible to see the comedy in a particular incident because the stress of the moment is so great. But the comedy is there, sometimes as humor expressed in a ludicrous reaction.

Danny's illness began to manifest itself at the end of the hippie era which, I believe, is what caused him to wear a bandanna and grow a long beard. He seldom took the bandanna off, and whenever my husband and I took him out to dinner, it was a constant battle. "Please take off the kerchief. You will look better," we would plead. The bandanna seemed to draw more attention to his illness since his combination of clothes was never the best. This bandanna problem went on for about nine years, and at times we did not take him to better restaurants if he didn't cooperate.

Then one day I went alone to take him out to a nearby coffee shop. When I arrived at the hospital, Danny was waiting in the lobby. He stood up to greet me, and as he walked towards me, I couldn't believe what I was seeing.

No bandanna—and no hair! He had had his hair shaven off completely, and his beard was a scary contrast.

Suddenly, I blurted out, "Put on your kerchief!"

I couldn't believe what I was saying.

Despair and anxiety smother the saving grace of humor. It is understandable that families, and particularly parents, who are so close to the problems of chronic mental illness are unable to see anything funny in particular situations. However, as time goes on and the problems of the illness are accepted, families will find themselves looking back on some incidents with an understanding chuckle or with a wry smile.

It was early afternoon on a warm spring day when I received a call from the state hospital telling me to be careful as my son Danny had just left there, making threats on my life. My instructions were to call the police if he came to the door. The police had already been notified of the threats.

My reactions at this time were not exactly normal since I was going through additional turmoil, being recently separated from my husband. (We have since reconciled.) Shaking, I ran across the street to a neighbor's house to call a friend. I wanted to be out of the house while I was on the phone.

I was there only about a minute when there was a loud knock on the door. I jumped a few inches from the floor and screamed, "Aaaaaah!" My neighbor opened the door to the water meter man taking his routine readings. I pretended nothing had happened as she greeted him. I stayed with my neighbor for about half an hour and then decided that since I had to eventually go home, I might as well do it now. I tried to muster up some courage but could find none in me.

I began to pace my kitchen floor, trying to put my thoughts together. Soon the meter man finished his readings on one end of the street and was now at my door. But I didn't know it was him. Again, the loud knock, and I screamed, "Aaaaah!" I quickly composed myself as I opened the door. I said not a word about my unusual reaction, and neither did he. (During this period it was still hard for me to tell anyone about the tragedy in my family.)

As he went down into the cellar, I noticed one side of his face was paralyzed. When he came back up, I asked him if he had Bell's Palsy since I was afflicted with it at one time and was familiar with it. "Yes," he said and immediately asked me quite a few questions about that. He left a few minutes later, with me wishing him well.

Again my mind returned to my problem when suddenly there was another loud knock on the door. I screamed even louder now. "AAAAAAH!" I sounded like I was shell-shocked.

"It's me again," said the meter man in a gentle voice, trying to calm me. "Just one more question that I forgot."

I let him in and said nothing about my strange behavior. To this day I wonder what he must have thought of me.

The roller coaster of emotions experienced by parents as they live through, and manage to survive, the escapades of their mentally ill children is testament to the endurance of the human spirit. The anxiety giving way to a flood of relief is indeed a traumatic experience. But the relief makes it bearable, and when relief is leavened with a sense of humor—or at least a wry appreciation of the circumstances—the healing of the trauma becomes stronger and more lasting.

Jean had a meeting with her counselor at the drop-in center at 10 o'clock in the morning. She had a family meeting the night before that had upset her. Her father was to pick her up later in the afternoon. When he arrived at the center, some of the other clients said Jean had left quite a while ago and had been crying. At first we thought she might be visiting one of her friends. I called everyone I knew. Her brother and sister went out looking for her. She was nowhere to be found. This was not like her. She always called home if she was going to be late. We didn't know what to do. It was getting dark. We called the police and were told there was nothing they could do until she had been missing for 24 hours. All night we waited. By morning we were all crazy with worry. Still no Jean. At 10 o'clock her sister and I took Jean's picture to the police station. They would put a description of her and what she was wearing over the police radio. All we could do was wait.

That afternoon, sitting by the telephone, I was thinking Jean had no clothes or money with her. I decided to call the bank to see if she had taken any of her money out of her account. At first they said they couldn't tell me because it was against regulations to give out such information. After talking to—and screaming at—three different people, I found out that she had taken her money out. Now I had a new worry. If she had money, she probably left town. On the third day of Jean's disappearance, I finally went to bed about 6:30 in the morning. At eight o'clock the telephone rang. My daughter leaped out of bed with a loud scream and answered the phone. It was a wrong number. My daughter had screamed because somehow she had twisted her neck and was in a lot of pain. I called a cab and took her to the hospital where a doctor in the emergency room put a collar on her neck. Then we rushed home to stay by the telephone.

On the fourth day, late in the afternoon, the phone rang. It was the manager of a hotel a few miles from where we lived. He asked if I was Jean's mother. When I said yes, he told me she had been at the hotel for the past four days and that she was fine. He said a maid thought she heard Jean crying and reported it. He also told me she had been by herself, that she had loads of money, that she had her meals sent up to her room and had paid all her bill. The room was $98 a day.

My husband and son went with me to bring her home. When we arrived at the hotel, the manager met us and was just so nice. He took us up to Jean's room and opened the door with a pass key. There she was in this beautiful room, with music playing softly, sitting on the edge of the bed writing, in her own little world. I said, "Hi." She looked at me as though this was the most natural situation in the world and said, "Mom, isn't this a beautiful room? Maybe someday you could come and stay here." Her father said just the right thing, "I'll say this for you, you have lots of class. Come on, dear, the vacation is over." And home we went.

We were so happy to see her but we hoped she wouldn't plan to take many of these vacations.

After Jean had supper and was in bed, I remembered the manager saying that she had a big roll of money. The next morning I asked her about it. She said she went to the bank and took her money out. I presumed she wandered around for a while, forgot she had the money, then went to a second bank, a branch of the first one, and took out the same amount, which was all she had in her account. About a week later we got a letter from the bank saying she was overdrawn. That was where the extra money came from. She had gone to the bank twice. We gave the money back to the bank, which closed out that little episode—which I can laugh about now.

When a problem is either resolved or put to rest for a while, the family is able to look back on past events like a spectator viewing a play. Often, in retrospect, it is possible to find something to laugh about.

My son Danny was now living in an old run-down boarding house. It was probably as old as the town itself. At first when he moved there, he would see his father and me but, after three months or so, without any medication or community support, he withdrew into his room and would never answer his door. At times he would move from one room to another. When that happened, my only thought was that it was cheaper rent, leaving him more money for drugs—or maybe he felt that a change would make him better.

This particular evening when I arrived, I found he was living on the third floor, in an old attic room. I knocked on the door, hoping he would let me in. I longed to see him and to kiss him. As usual, he yelled at me and told me to leave and never come back. As I slipped his weekly money under the door I noticed a keyhole and tried to peek in, hoping to get a glimpse of him. Unable to see anything, I left.

Approaching my car, I turned to look up to see if there was at least a light on in his room. In doing so I saw an old fire escape which led up to a door next to his room. If I climbed up there, I thought, maybe I could see him. It was worth a try. I looked around and since no tenants were going in or out at the time I decided I would do it.

I had to be careful as it was a windy night and very dark, with only a small light shining on the back porch. I slowly got to the top. I found I could see into his room through the window if I leaned over a little. Now I had to be careful not to startle him. I know if I lived on the top floor and someone knocked or peeked in my window, I would jump out of my skin. I saw Danny sitting up in his bed staring at the wall. I softly called his name. There was absolutely no reaction. He didn't even look at me, just asked, "Ya! What do you want?"

After that it was only a one-way conversation. I spoke

quietly so no one below would hear me. I looked around his room, trying to see how he lived. I had been visiting for about 10 minutes when I became aware that I was slightly swaying with the breeze on this old fire escape. I decided I better leave before the wind picked up. "Goodbye, Danny," I said softly. "I love you. I'll visit again."

My legs felt very weak, and I had to feel for each step going down. I could barely see. I finally felt the ground and with a sigh of relief thought, "Thank goodness I didn't fall." It would sound so strange in a newspaper, especially since there was no fire, and I didn't even live there. Later I thought what a bizarre figure I must have been on that fire escape. And I had to laugh at myself.

Grasping at straws becomes second nature to the parents of a severely mentally ill son or daughter—even to clutching at humor under the blackest of circumstances. Fasten on to anything that may lighten the spirit; it becomes an almost automatic reaction.

Sometimes when it seems it isn't possible for things to get any worse, they do. My husband and I were finding our lives complicated with family, work and house problems. I had planned to meet him at a local restaurant for a bite to eat before an early meeting with our son David's counselor. I was early, entered the restaurant but returned immediately to my car to get a paper. I found my husband standing beside my car looking at the right rear tire which was flat and on the rim. It was the second flat tire in two days, which meant there wasn't any spare. He was very upset, and there was little I could say.

"Well, look at it this way," I finally said. "We've got a flat tire but there are still three good ones on the car."

Laughter, they say, is the best medicine. It heals the body, the mind and the soul. For the families of the long-term mentally ill, humor can have a priceless therapeutic value. Though families think they will never laugh again when they are first weighed down by the terrible emotional turmoil of a mentally ill member, they will learn that laughter, even a small chuckle or smile, can lift their spirits. Humor does abound, and it can be found in the most unexpected places at the most unexpected times.

One morning in early December I picked up Danny at the hospital and took him out for breakfast. We later did some Christmas shopping. He seemed to enjoy himself. When returning him to the hospital, his psychiatrist, Dr. Whitney, walked by and Danny excitedly called out, "Dr. Whitney, my mother and I went Christmas shopping, and I bought a Smurf pencil for my niece!"

"A what pencil?" questioned the doctor.

"Smurf," answered Danny.

"I don't know what a Smurf is," said the doctor and quickly walked away.

A puzzled look came across my face as I remarked, "That's funny, he doesn't know what a Smurf is."

Danny shook his head and replied, "He doesn't know anything about the outside world."

Chapter 9

Dreaming for the Future

This is the dream parents hold in their hearts: that one day their mentally ill loved ones will know the joy of work well done, of healthy laughter, of communication and rapport with friends, of concentration and physical coordination, of sleeping without fear and waking with hope. And when these parents consider the scientists and psychologists, psychiatrists and theologians working toward this end, they have some hope that one day the dream will be a reality—even if only after they are gone.

I closed my eyes. It was a quiet time of the day, and I wanted to rest. As soon as my head nestled on the pillow of my sofa, I began to dream. Two roads appeared before me, each beckoning me to explore. I turned to the road on my right and hurried along as my curiosity took over. Entering this road, I noticed a colorful sign on a post which read, "Road of Love." The air smelled sweetly of flowers, and the sun shown bright. This road was pretty and well taken care of. It made my walk very pleasant.

A small farm was just ahead, and it took me awhile to realize that the help were mentally ill as they functioned in almost normal fashion. They seemed happy, well-fed and thoroughly content as they tended the crops and animals with love. They were friendly and waved as I passed by. I soon came across a cluster of little houses. A resident in his early twenties was giving his home a second coat of paint. He noticed I appeared a little lost and smiled at me. He stopped his work and said he would be happy to show me his village. The first stop was his little home. It was simple but comfortable and decorated in his taste. In the middle of the village were many small businesses and activity centers. My young guide told me that the residents were proud of their village. For some it was a stop-over, for a few months or a few years, and for others their permanent residence, which became their way of life. Residents all looked after each other and there were many family get-togethers. It was freedom and protection molded together in strong stability. The staff members were dedicated to their work and were thoroughly qualified through education and experience.

My last stop was a building called Village Town Hall. At this point I thanked my friend and told him I would manage my way back by myself after checking in here. Upon entering I noticed clerks busying themselves with paper work and some people mingling about. Plaques on the walls told a brief history of its beginning. I decided to stay awhile and read the various pamphlets about this village.

I was so engrossed with this newfound program that I barely heard the voice of my beloved son Danny calling out, "Mom!" I turned to see him being checked in as a new resident. My heart overflowed with joy. We embraced and chatted awhile. He said he would call me to give me his address and would soon be home to visit.

I began my journey back home with enormous energy and warmed with hope. As I turned, I felt a tug at my skirt and a voice called out, "Don't forget the other road." How could anything be better than the road I was just on, I thought, but decided to find out anyway.

As I turned on to the other road, my dreaming became a nightmare. I saw a dismal looking sign designating the "Road of Ugliness." A police car was picking up a mentally ill girl in a department store, probably for causing too much disturbance, I thought. The policeman looked tired. It seemed to be a constant call. The air became strangely still and extremely cold. I began to hurry my steps. Down the road a bit I saw a "bag lady" huddled in a doorway, trying to keep out of the elements. She used her bag, her only possession, as her pillow. A shiver went up my spine, and I pulled my own coat up around my neck. I began to look for some sign of hope but could find none.

A car slowly came to a stop, and a woman was dropping off her friend. She helped her out of the car, and I could hear their conversation. The friend's son was wandering the countryside looking for a place where he would not be harassed. She knew his search would be fruitless as he was very ill. She walked up to her door, and as she turned to her friend, I noticed that her sadness overpowered her pretty smile.

Not too far from this home was another home filled with distress. A daughter was going through a crisis, hallucinating with strange conversations. I could see members of her family arguing with each other, not knowing which direction to take.

What a terrible road, I thought, and with not a moment's peace. Hysterical laughter seemed to follow me. I came upon a boarding house and saw a disturbed person sitting on his bed, smoking marijuana and talking to the wall. During his conversation, his laughter would ring out. Outside his door were con artists ready to sell drugs to him or steal anything of value if he left his room. Suddenly I remembered this was the boarding house Danny was living in. He would never answer when I knocked, and I had to slip his weekly money under his door, hoping each time it would not be stolen again. I decided to check on him. He was not there, and when I asked the landlord, he told me Danny had just left and gave no forwarding address. My son had recently been discharged from the hospital because he was not participating in any of the programs or taking medication. "Oh, dear God, please send me back to the other road," I pleaded.

"There is never any end to this one." After my desperate prayer, I decided to go to the police station and report my son missing. I entered on the side of the courthouse and saw a distraught mother who had filed a complaint to have her mentally ill son arrested because he had been breaking into her home. It was her only way to get him readmitted to the hospital for help. When the police brought her son in, she almost fainted.

I fled from this horrible scene and came upon a church where I could find some refuge for a while. Inside were many people all dressed in black. A homeless mentally ill man had passed away and was being prayed over before burial. His physical health had completely broken down from constantly being bussed by communities from one part of the country to another. The strange behavior of the mentally ill on the streets had become unacceptable to society and in our "progress" we had adopted "Greyhound therapy." Tears streamed down my cheeks.

How can all this happen in a land so great? Have we in turn gone mad? To cope with life is so hard for normal people, how can one with severe thought disorder possibly survive deinstitutionalization in this manner with so much prejudice against them? I began to panic. It seemed that I would be on this road with my son forever. I wanted desperately to go back to the other one, but each time I took a step there was an obstacle.

I felt the tug at my skirt again and with disgust said, "Oh, you again. I never should have listened to you for now I'm not able to go back to the Road of Love. There is no hope." The voice replied, "Walk on. Never give up. Eventually you'll get on that road again." With that, a ray of sunlight burst out from behind the clouds. I bowed my head and beneath my feet a budding rose appeared, my sign of hope.

Parents of chronically mentally ill children die as do all parents—and the children live on. Only some few will recover from their illness. What is to become of these people is a major concern of all afflicted families.

I guess I have taken it for granted that when I am gone, Lora will continue to live at the state hospital quarter-way house, taken care of as she is now, which is neither very bad nor very good. I expect that her three brothers will visit her occasionally, but they live out of the state and have their own lives and responsibilities, even though they are concerned about her. They will not be visiting her every week as I do. And that does bother me because then I see my daughter as a lone, helpless person, almost totally dependent on people who may not have her best interests at heart. She can be very arrogant and abrasive as she goes through a schizophrenic cycle, and though she has been fortunate in having therapists who are sympathetic and understanding, that may not always be the case.

I guess, when I stop to think about it, I am always praying in the back of my mind that I will have some good stroke of fortune that will make it possible for me to see that Lora is set permanently in the best possible living circumstances. I think about buying a big house, with land around it, in a pleasant town where my daughter and perhaps four or five others who are chronically mentally ill could live, each with a private room, where they could spend their days to some purpose, involved in work or hobbies that interest them, eating healthful foods, all this happening under the supervision of a small but dedicated live-in staff. It's only a dream but perhaps someday . . .

These concerns go to the very heart of every parent of a mentally ill loved one.

As I sit at my desk and ponder my daughter Jean's future, the tears keep getting in the way of my writing. As her mother, I know how difficult it is for her to relate to people, that most of the time she doesn't remember things, that she doesn't eat a balanced meal, that most of the time she eats junk food. She is dependent on other people for her medication because she is afraid to take it on her own, and she sometimes forgets.

Although the staff at the community house where Jean lives are trying to let her fend for herself in everyday living, very little progress is being made. We worry very much about her inability to cope or fully care for herself. After we're gone who will look after her needs? Will her brother, sister, or friends go to see her once a week as we do?

Our hopes are that someday God will hear our prayers and a miracle will happen. In the meantime, we dream that in the near future Jean and other chronically mentally ill people who live in community houses can have their own rooms and things to do besides sitting around idle all day.

The basic accepted psychiatric approach in this country has spawned an appalling bureaucracy of mental health professionals who are almost totally ineffective. They mainly follow accepted practices that, in effect, keep the mentally ill in the state of being patients, with little thought or hope of improving their condition beyond a manageable point. And yet, with patience and persistence, families can have an impact on professional attitudes and programs. And they are doubly fortunate if they have involvement with professionals who can see beyond the established systems.

During the 15 years since Lora's first schizophrenic break, she has achieved a measure of normalcy and self-confidence only when I forced the issue or the professionals working with her broke with tradition and dared to do something outside the conventional program.

One of the happiest years of her life was when she was at the Psychiatric Institute in New York City shortly after her first break. The Institute focused on creative young people. After they were there for a period of some months, patients were allowed—I should say encouraged—to go into the city each day and pursue their careers. They returned to the Institute at night where they were secure and cherished. Lora, who was trained as an actress, dancer, and choreographer, went out and did her thing. She choreographed a piece, trained a six-dancer company, oversaw costumes and the set, and presented the dance on a program at the Cubiculo Theater. It was an extrordinary accomplishment. Unfortunately, patients stay at the Psychiatric Institute for only 18 months. When Lora had to leave, she was devastated.

Several years later, while she was at a state hospital in Massachusetts, Lora reached one of her periodic, saner plateaus and announced she was leaving to get a job. Since she had always been a voluntary patient, she was allowed to go. She went into Boston, got a room at the "Y" and perused the want ads. One advertisement was seeking dancers for a company. Lora reasoned that if dancers were wanted, a choreographer was needed also. She called the telephone number in the ad and actually sold the woman the idea of hiring her as the company choreographer. At this writing, a little more than a year later, Lora is still the choreographer and assistant director of the company.

But it wasn't easy. No matter how well Lora did professionally, she was still a schizophrenic and needed support and understanding to give her the sense of security she required if she was going to live in the community. The system to provide it was not there. Unable to cope, Lora gave up her room in the community and went back to the hospital, even though she loved her job and did well at it.

I refused to let the matter rest there. Her work was too important to Lora to let it go down the drain. Over the years I had been very vocal about the need for the system to bend to the needs of the patients. I believe that with support and encouragement many patients can do much more than they are required to do—not all, but many. For the most part, they are intelligent adults with many talents. The simple sheltered workshop type of labor they are given is an insult to their intelligence, and some refuse to do it, including Lora. When she went back to the hospital, the staff didn't know what to do with her. To her therapist I bemoaned the fact that Lora wasn't at the Psychiatric Institute where she would be allowed to go to her work and return to the hospital at the end of the day, which had been an ideal support system.

Well, I must give credit to the staff and consulting psychiatrist. They met, discussed the situation and alternatives and agreed to try to recreate for Lora the Psychiatric Institute experience. This was remarkable, especially since Lora's job was a long bus and subway ride away from the hospital. The kind, understanding woman who owned the dance company was contacted and said she wanted Lora to come back because she was an excellent teacher. It was part-time work because the dancers also held regular daytime jobs, so Lora was able to make the trip once or twice a week, as was necessary. It was an outstanding example of professionals stepping outside the bounds of the rigid system to help a patient achieve personal and professional satisfaction.

Lora's experience brings out two important points. Mentally ill people need strong support systems, and they need fulfilling, satisfying work that restores their self-confidence and self-respect.

Support systems must be in place before any real achievements can be fostered. When a mentally ill person is ready to leave the hospital or a quarter-way or half-way house, he or she must have adequate support in the community in order to adjust. It is unrealistic to expect a chronically mentally ill person to have the ability to cope without the proper support.

One of the most practical kinds of support is financial. For the mentally ill especially some sense of financial security helps them maintain self-respect and dignity. When young people are struck down with chronic mental illness, they can seldom work for an extended period to support themselves. Many families cannot carry the long-term burden of providing their mentally ill member with money for basic needs, clothing, and perhaps a little entertainment. This then becomes a problem for society. It is generally necessary for some government agency to make provisions for the mentally ill so that they can have the necessities of life. In the United States a national program of income-maintenance called Supplementary Security Income (SSI) provides a monthly cash allowance for the needy who are aged, physically or mentally impaired or blind and are unable to maintain gainful employment.

One may still maintain a home, a car, burial insurance, small savings and some personal goods and still be eligible for SSI benefits. It is necessary to have proof of low income for a period prior to application. Pay stubs will provide evidence of a low income. The applicant must submit any bank books and/or bank statements for review and report any financial assets. Also, it is necessary to have proof of citizenship and physicians' statements regarding health. Testimony of a relative regarding these facts is not sufficient. Application for SSI is made at the local Social Security Administration office.

When a person is eligible for SSI, he or she is automatically eligible for Medicaid assistance, a program which pays for medical, hospital care and physicians' fees. All fees are paid directly to the services by the program. The rates are determined by the state's Rate Setting Commission on a "reasonable cost" basis. Funding for Medicaid is shared by the federal and state governments. The client pays nothing for services within the program's parameters; services vary from state to state. It is possible for the client to return to work and still receive benefits until it is deter-

mined officially that he can support himself. The Supplemental Security Income program is not part of the Social
Security program.

The Founding Fathers did not guarantee the right of
everyone to health care when they wrote the U.S. Constitution. It is only in the last few decades that a determined
effort has been made by the government to insure medical
and hospital care for the aged and disabled. A first step
came in the form of the Medicare employer-employee
shared insurance plan as part of the Social Security program. Under the program, those over 65, or at any age if
disabled, blind or suffering from chronic renal disease, who
have contributed to the Social Security Fund with payroll
deductions and have earned sufficient "work credits" to be
insured, are eligible for Social Security Disability Income
(SSDI).[6]

When applying for SSDI, it is helpful for the applicant to have his or her Social Security number at hand,
proof of age, medical records, and, if possible, statements
from doctors, as well as names and locations of work places.
There are no low income requirements when applying for
Social Security Disability entitlements.

If a person is determined to be disabled by the Disability Determination Service,[7] he is eligible under the SSDI
program to receive monthly checks five months from the
onset of the disability, the first day of the sixth month. Payments may be retroactive one year from the month of filing if the onset was 18 months earlier. Medicare
entitlements, the Social Security insurance program for the
disabled, begin 24 months after the start of the disability
checks and help to cover hospital, medical and physicians'
fees.[8]

In spite of all the advocacy and legal efforts, there still
are not funds available for adequate care of the severely

handicapped indigent population. Services vary from state to state, and eligibility requirements for some programs vary also. If family funds are limited, it is not unwarranted for parents to consider moving to a state which provides the best benefits for the care of a mentally ill son or daughter, in or near an area where access to quality care is available and where there is a good patient-to-qualified-staff ratio.

The need for freedom from stress makes it clear that environment and supportive programs are of prime importance to ensure improvement for the mentally ill. In fact, that was recognized and provided in ancient Greece. One of the first medical centers in history was founded in Epidauros by the minor Greek god Asklipios who preceded Hippocrates. (In ancient and even modern Greece, myth and reality flow into each other.) Worshipped as a healer, Asklipios believed that to cure mental illness, or any ailment, it was necessary to put the patient in serene, harmonious surroundings. He selected the most beautiful site he could find, an Eden-like spot of soft rolling hills, flowers and trees. And he built not only medical buildings but an extraordinary amphitheater where choral groups performed, poets declaimed and drama groups performed for the patients. Asklipios believed it was as necessary to treat the soul as the mind.

In the 1800s a similar approach, but to a lesser degree, was made in the United States. Those concerned with the welfare of the mentally ill took over vast tracts of land in the countryside and constructed many-building hospitals called asylums, a place of haven. The word asylum comes from the Greek word *asulon,* meaning sanctuary. It was a thread leading back to the ideas of Asklipios. At the asylums, patients worked with farm animals, cultivated gardens and lived a protected back-to-nature life.

Unfortunately, over the years the altruistic, idyllic concept degenerated. Patients who worked on the state-run farms were described as slave labor by concerned citizens. The hospitals themselves became warehouses for the unwanted. It was a terrible commentary on "progress"— as the country grew in material wealth and knowledge, it had less and less concern for the mentally ill.

Today there is a reversal in this attitude. Patients are being deinstitutionalized but, sadly, they are descending upon communities that are not prepared to give them the support and programs they so desperately need. So they are, in effect, being re-institutionalized in the community, consigned to mental ghettos where they often live in substandard housing and roam the streets. When they do socialize, it is only with other mentally ill patients. They are far from being integrated into the community, which was the intent of deinstitutionalization.

So-called mental health experts in this country might do well to look at the communities for the chronically mentally ill in some European countries where patients live a kind of life very similar to that envisioned by the good people of the nineteenth century, who fostered the idea of asylums in the true sense of that word.

The need for half-way houses and protected group living situations is enormous. Many chronically mentally ill people do not need to be hospitalized. They *do* need to live in an environment that is comfortable, protected, and free from stress. Sometimes the family can provide such a setting, but more often the stresses of family living make the illness more severe.

Support and supervision are the most important ingredients to successful community living for the mentally ill. Once they leave the hospital and are on their own— in a half-way house, a room or a cooperative apartment—

the tasks of daily living can become bewildering. To expect the mentally ill to make it on their own in the community without a program that offers total support is expecting the impossible.

A good model of public community support exists in Madison, Wisconsin. Known as the *Program for Assertive Community Treatment (PACT)*, it operates from a central location which is staffed 24 hours a day. A psychiatrist and other staff members work with the released patients in their residences and in places of employment and, in general, help them adjust to community living. Staff members assist them with food shopping and other basic necessities. They also inspect the patients' residences on a regular basis. If the patient has a problem any time of day or night, there is always someone available to help. If there is any doubt that the patient is taking medication properly, the staff takes steps to see that he adheres to his medication regime. The PACT program is a big step forward.

It is important to select a half-way house that provides the programs and professional staff, as well as a residence, that is suitable for the individual patient. For instance, a mentally ill person who needs 24-hour supervision would be better served in a facility that has a psychiatrist on the premises.

Parkland Place in Birmingham, Alabama, for example, is staffed by medical professionals, registered nurses, registered occupational therapists and mental health technologists. A mental health technician is one who has earned a comparatively new degree in counseling oriented toward families and communities. At Parkland a great deal of emphasis is put on individualized treatment and training in what they call "patienthood." This is teaching the residents what their rights are and what their responsibilities are as well.

At *Hawthorne Apartments* in Eugene, Oregon, it is interesting to note that the management is not medical, and a resident manager lives on the premises. Case managers are mainly responsible for the care of the residents, 60 percent of whom are of high functioning level and only 10 percent of low functioning level. Applicants benefit who have a "significant other." The management believes that those who have the support of a friend, parent, or other relative have a more encouraging prognosis. They have also introduced the use of a "residents' friend," who is a client and serves as a role model and counselor, one who can be depended upon to help in emergencies. Funding of half-way houses is the primary hurdle in establishing any facility. In the case of Hawthorne, it was the coordinated assistance of families, advocates, the residential provider, builders, and the state division of HUD that brought the project to fruition.

Fountain House Club in New York City is the most loosely administered of the three examples given here, but it contributes enormously to the needs of the mentally ill in that city. The dominant theme throughout the Fountain House activities is that the organization is a club and not a residence for mentally ill people. Half-way houses are sprinkled throughout the city, and every applicant must show an interest in using the clubhouse to be accepted for a residency. There is only a part-time psychiatrist employed for emergencies but the city clinics and hospitals are available when necessary, and every program at Fountain House provides contact with professionals.

If a client loses his job, goes through a cycle of distress or needs a change of medication, he receives attention at the club. Every member is assured housing and work. Training may begin with a prevocational course and transitional program before obtaining full-time work with a regular pay scale. Sometimes two men or two women will share one position or a group will work together. Employers are not permitted to lower their standards or their pay scale, and there is no subsidy by Fountain House. Past work history or hospitalizations are not a consideration for employment. There are no job interview ratings, and motivation is not an issue. Failures occur and are worked through.[9]

There is much to do before half-way houses become a reality in all communities but it is not an unrealistic goal. Properly operated, half-way houses represent the best possible living situation for great numbers of the chronically mentally ill.

Chapter 10

How Can We Change Things Now?

One percent of the population of the United States has schizophrenia, which translates into almost three million people, affecting about 15 million family members. The United States census shows an overall population increase of 9,500,000 people between 1980 and 1985. At this rate, and at the increasing rate of inflation, it is easy to see the calamity that may befall the mentally ill as various government services compete for the tax dollar.

If families have the spirit to take steps now, they may be able to forestall a catastrophe. Funds for the mentally handicapped are allocated by legislators, many of whom have little experience in the field of mental illness, though they may be well intentioned. We, the families, can support and encourage those legislators who take an active part in improving conditions for the mentally ill. We must become informed about the budgetary process and not be overwhelmed by the enormity of the subject. At the same time we can feed information to the state committee members whose time is limited and whose desks are piled high. As you sift through the mountain of printed material that is published by organizations, newspapers, state and federal programs regarding the mentally ill, underline the

pertinent data with a color-pen and hand it to your legislators or committee members the next time you meet them.
They'll appreciate the fact that you took the time to under-
score the important information.

We need to change a system that tolerates waste in
antiquated facilities, duplication of clerical functions and
excessive use of expensive technological equipment. While
new courthouses and administration buildings are rising,
the mental hospitals are deteriorating. Heating systems are
antiquated. Toilets are leaking and running endlessly. Roofs
need repair. There is inefficient duplication of staff. Some
hospitals are overstaffed while at the same time others are
short of personnel. Employees at the low end of the wage
scale complain of being underpaid, and this results in a
high rate of turnover and costly training of new personnel.
Ken Jacobsen of the Alliance for the Mentally Ill in Mult-
nomah County, Oregon, pinpointed this issue in their February 1984 newsletter when he stated, "We need to ask
what effect administrative issues have on the practical face-
to-face client treatment at the end of the chain."

Fortunately, there are people throughout this country
who refuse to abandon the fate of the mentally ill to the
"system." Many of these people are parents, and the motivation to act comes in many ways and in various circumstances. Often parents will find they are dealing with
professionals outside the mental health field. These
encounters can be amiable, with understanding on both
sides, but it becomes frustrating indeed when the professional feels he has to be adamant on a subject.

As I was sitting in the courtroom waiting for my case to
be heard, my mind flashed back to an earlier time when I
had come here after filing an application for a restraining
order against my son Danny after he broke into my home

several times. I was appearing before the judge to explain the situation.

I felt so comfortable with that particular judge. I sensed his warmness right away, and because of this I began to weep. When I finished telling him my story, in between tears, he smiled and said he would give me a restraining order good for six months, stating my son was to stay away from my house and to keep away from me. This was a relief and yet too harsh. I told the judge I found it hard to explain my son's illness and that I still wanted to see him and could he please word the order differently. He understood, and taking his time, he jotted down different words and came up with an added sentence that pleased us both.

Reading the addition at a later date, I also found it amusing. It read, "Petitioner hereby notifies the Respondent that at any time he may so request, she is desirous of visiting him, as soon as she possibly is able to, wherever he may be."

My mind was suddenly jolted to the present as I heard the court officer announce the entrance of the presiding judge. I quickly rose to my feet. While sitting there, listening to the cases before mine, I observed the sternness of this judge and his business-like manner and foresaw a battle ahead for me.

When I stood before him, I explained I had a restraining order and since Danny had broken that order, he had been readmitted to the hospital. Now that the six months was ready to expire, I wished him to renew it for at least a year or indefinitely, until my son improved, since coming back and forth to the court would hinder my health and possibly disturb my son even more.

The judge read the existing order, then looked at me and said that what I asked could not be done according to the law. I would have to wait for my son to break into the house again and then apply for another restraining order.

"Your Honor," I said, "since this is an unusual case, why can't you make an exception?"

"Ma'am, that is the law!" he replied in a strong voice.

I thought to myself, can't this judge, who must be intelligent, realize that there is a good chance a restraining order need not be renewed when issued to a mentally stable person but it would be different with a schizophrenic? I decided to try again.

"But Your Honor," I said, "it would be easier for me to get help if I have a restraining order in effect."

"Ma'am, that cannot be done!" His voice was harsher now.

Out of the corner of my eye I could see the court officer move closer behind me. I guess he felt the judge would soon cite me for contempt. I knew I was not going to win but I still had to speak.

"It's not going to hurt anybody if it's renewed," I said. The judge just looked at me. "Oh well, thank you anyway," I mumbled. "I guess now people will just have to band together and change some laws."

The judge gave me a weak smile and wished me luck. At this point I think he was anxious to get rid of me.

Another situation that can bring parents to court is the question of guardianship. This is a complicated and sticky issue. When parents become legal guardians of a mentally ill adult child, it does not necessarily follow that they have the power to demand medication or specific treatments. Each state has its own legislation that may block or frustrate parents in their search for care they feel will be more effective. And there are instances when judges may have a view different than that of the parents and so refuse the parents' requests. Some judges in Massachusetts have advised parents that guardianship papers must spell out specifically the powers the parents want.

For instance, if parents seek to have the power to authorize medication, a general guardianship is worth nothing. The power to insist on medication for the patient must be spelled out in the papers. Parents would do well to consult with a lawyer before undertaking guardianship steps. In many states there are organizations of lawyers especially interested in helping families with legal problems related to the mentally ill. Remember, the road to guardianship can be long and expensive.

My wife and I became co-guardians of our son David because we thought it was the only way to save his life. He had been diagnosed schizophrenic and was wandering the countryside. We were supported in this decision by close friends whose family had committed a son as their "only hope of saving him." They were successful.

The returns are not in yet in the case of David. The guardianship and the involuntary admission were six years ago. There were a number of times during this period when we expressed the feeling that we would not counsel anyone else to follow our course knowing what we know today. The legal paper we possess did not persuade one doctor to prescribe medication for our son at home although it had been helpful in the hospital. Neither did we receive an explanation for this doctor's lack of cooperation. Our hard-earned authority as guardians did not permit us to testify at our son's commitment hearing. It has never allowed us to see our son's records or have control of his money.

Another legal matter that requires careful consideration is the subject of wills. Several questions arise. The basic one is how best to care for the mentally ill child when the parents are gone. And then, how will the settlement of the estate, large or small, affect the family? Also, how would the will affect government payments presently received by the mentally ill child? Families with chronically disabled children do not serve them well if they do not leave a will specifying how they want their property divided. The urgency for providing a will and considering the establishment of a trust, even a small one, is very real.

When there is no such legal document in existence, the court steps in as executor and distributes the assets according to the law but only after the payment of debts, fees, and taxes. This frequently requires the liquidation of property, much to the dissatisfaction of the heirs. If a mentally disabled loved one receives an equal share according to the will and if it exceeds the "needs base," then he will lose his eligibility for services which the state and federal governments provide. This could mean a loss of hundred of thousands of dollars over a life span and place a heavy burden of care on the survivors.

Loss of eligibility of state and federal funds may not be a consideration for everyone. One couple, for instance, has decided that out of a sense of fairness to all, their estate should be shared equally among their children even though one may be completely irresponsible. Their reasoning is that if he dissipates his inheritance, he will have to manage as best he can without relying on his brothers and sisters for rescue. They feel that permitting him this freedom might turn things around, teaching him how to handle his money. And there are other attitudes.

> *My husband and* I are making no demands on the brothers and sisters of our ill son David. We cannot measure what problems they would face if they had full responsibility for their brother. Would a schism develop within their families, between their families? With so many unknowns, how can we put the burden on them?
>
> We have explained to the two boys that we are planning to have a third party as a trustee to handle their brother's affairs through a trust, with their right to dismissal. The boys must decide for themselves how much responsibility

they will assume for their sick brother. Their relationships will vary from time to time, sometimes closer, sometimes more distant, depending upon how responsive their ill brother is.

Where will the mentally disabled live when their parents are gone? Will the state give them the care they need? Knowing how little community housing exists today for the mentally ill and that much of it is substandard, families have initiated an extraordinary trend across the country. They are banding together as corporations, or are working through their Alliance groups, to buy property and create their own housing facilities for the mentally ill in their areas. Often they are able to get funds and other support for their projects from federal and state agencies. At this writing there are about a dozen such groups, from Oregon to Massachusetts. It takes a lot of dedication and hard work for parents to take on the role of housing entrepreneur, but the satisfactions make it worthwhile.

In St. Louis, Susan M. Hecker[10] and others worked to transform an old house into a community support system which grew until today they also have an apartment building with 19 efficiency units, as well as additional units leased elsewhere for the chronically mentally ill. This is a striking example of what one woman can organize and accomplish. Mrs. Hecker didn't realize when she first sought books and journals on mental illness that she was breaking ground for the first aftercare residence in her state. She recalls that there were telephone calls and visits to state facilities. Reading material from complexes like Fountain House, Horizon House, Lexington House and others filled her shelves. It was not unusual for her to meet others with similar family concerns, but it was exceptional that three years later six couples matched her courage and together they embarked on a project that produced a community-supported rehabilitation center with programs to motivate and nurture mentally ill members. Financial status was not a consideration for eligibility. Its name, symbolizing the spirit and the goal of the program, was to be Independence Center.

But first Susan Hecker developed expertise. She received some formal training in community support for long-term chronic patients. She learned all she could from educators and professionals. She sought assistance from members of her chapter of the Alliance for the Mentally Ill, the American Schizophrenic Society of Bio-Chemistry, and groups associated with mental retardation. She cultivated people who could advise her on the advantages of a tax-exempt corporation and attended seminars on the art of fund raising. She formed an alliance with the local university and later a managing contract with the same institution. All those who work for change would do well to take a lesson from Susan Hecker.

Advocates for change dare not leave the answer to the problem of aftercare for the mentally ill entirely to the state. It is not possible to trust government to provide homes for those who are ill if there are not existing appropriate facilities. Most families are not equipped psychologically or financially, nor are they sufficiently knowledgeable, to maintain a severely mentally handicapped adult at home. There is a pressing need for residences that will provide a safe and nurturing environment, and differences must be taken into account. Not all the mentally ill have the same requirements. Some respond better than others and have greater potential. Some are more optimistic, have more will to recover. Perhaps some have more faith, while others are negative and less hopeful.

It is not easy for laymen to walk in the shoes of the

parents of a mentally ill child. Those who have not experienced the terrible trauma of severe mental illness in their families are apt to say to themselves, "If only they had given that child a little more TLC, we wouldn't have crowded mental hospitals today." Or, regarding the young schizophrenics, they might think, "If only they had more willpower, they could pull themselves out of this dilemma." "Why don't they stay in one job? Why do they go from one job to another?" "Their parents weren't strict enough." "Their parents were too strict." The families of the mentally ill must educate the public, even as they themselves are being educated. It is incumbent upon the families to become experts in the matters of mental illness, to learn how providers, such as aftercare and drop-in centers, clinics, half-way houses, and food contractors, operate and to understand budgets, if they are to achieve the care they wish for their ill children.

Today the climate for improving conditions is better than it was 10 or 20 years ago. More professionals are looking to the community for help and are encouraging advocacy. There is opportunity now for change. At their budget and executive meetings, representatives in the government are noticing the presence of members of the Alliance for the Mentally Ill. The legislators are listening to the voices of families who are becoming involved in hospital programs, aftercare services, sharing groups and the legislative process. Today the livelihood of the chronic mentally ill is almost entirely dependent upon the legislation that controls government money. The government is the prime provider but the citizen is its employer. It is important for families to develop a background of expertise, to form opinions and make educated decisions—all the way to the voting booth.

Contacting legislators is simple and effective in moving legislation from the Docket Book to the floor. When someone from a home district calls the State House, the politicians take notice. But where to start?

You will hear a conversation or a report on television or read about a proposed bill. You might visit your State House and scan the Docket Book where all the proposed bills are registered. By law this list is open to the public. Once you have decided whether or not you wish to support a bill, it is appropriate to write a letter or call a member of the appropriate committee or your representative or senator, and state your position. For many of us, a trip to the State House is not convenient. Then we may go to the telephone directory and look up the listing, first under the state designation, e.g., Massachusetts, Commonwealth of; then the sublisting, Legislative branch; next House of Representatives or Senate. There you will probably find a number for General Information and for Clerk. With a direct call to the Clerk and a brief description of the bill, you may obtain the Docket number if you do not have it and discern the location of a bill on its journey to the floor of one of the branches of the legislature. The Clerk may say, "The committee is considering it now," or "It has moved to the Ways and Means Committee," or "It has been reported favorably out of Ways and Means and has gone to the floor of the House of Representatives or the Senate for a reading." Telephone calls and letters help to keep good things alive and also nip legislation you oppose.

Having called the Clerk, what next? Another telephone call will bring the committee member's secretary to the phone. You might begin, "Hello, this is Mrs. Copeland. I'd like to ask Representative Smart to vote for the bill for accreditation of mental hospitals." Occasionally the secretary will ask why. If you wish, you may give a reason. In any case, the secretary will undoubtedly make a note of your position and thank you for calling. With an equally courteous farewell, the mission is completed and has added leverage for better care for "our kids."

Anyone may offer a bill but it is not likely to be given much attention unless it is processed through a member of the legislature. The Clerk lists the bill in the Docket Book, assigns a number to it and sends it to the appropriate committee. You may attend a committee's public hearing and, if you wish, give testimony in defense or opposition to a bill. Sometimes you are required to sign up at a prior time to be heard. Legislators are responsive to personal experiences told in absolute honesty and are impatient with exaggerations, contradictions and long philosophical opinions. You may not see all the results of your efforts but others may benefit from them in the future.

There is a saying, "If wishes were horses, beggars might ride." Well, there isn't any free ride for the advocates for the mentally ill. Dreams must be put on hold. Families must roll up their sleeves and go to work to rally all possible resources if they want a better support system for their children. When chronic mental illness strikes, families can turn to the medical, psychiatric and social service professionals and to friends. But in the final analysis it is the family members seeking solutions to problems they share who stand together and reach out beyond their personal places to improve local and state services for the mentally ill.

Chapter 11

Reaching Out Through Networking

For the human problems that families of the psychiatrically disabled face, there are no easy answers. But there is an alternative to coping alone. Families are joining together in their local communities and areas to offer each other support and understanding. Meeting in homes, churches, libraries and other community settings, these networks of linked individuals can find hope and the personal support they need. The understanding and help of others who have gone through similar experiences provide the essential ingredients of self-help, which leads to mutual support and networking.

> *My journey before* the founding of our group, the Alliance for the Mentally Ill of Middlesex County (MA), and before I became a member, was extremely painful. It still is, but there are more rest periods and support.
>
> When mental illness first struck our home, it was utter chaos. Everyone was confused and seemed to be running in different directions. The mounting feelings of disbelief, anger, guilt, and despair were all bound up and ready to erupt. It was the end without the ending. No one in the family could really offer support to another, which resulted in each person's escaping to his own corner to cope alone.

Whatever effort was put out seemed to be a complete waste, thus causing everyone to just give up.

Looking back, I don't know how I survived the days when Danny was living at home. It is impossible to live with a person who has chronic mental illness. They take over the house and your life. Danny kept topsy-turvy hours, carried on senseless conversations, laughed hysterically or, going to the other extreme, spent day after day in bed. Only another who has gone through it can understand, and no amount of explanation would suffice for one who hasn't.

Then a change occurred in my life. My social outreach worker suggested I visit a group of families who were meeting once a week to talk about mental illness. My husband and I attended, hoping for the unreasonable—that a magic cure for schizophrenia would make this very bad dream go away. Unfortunately, my husband felt it was futile to partic-ipate in the meetings after he learned there was no magic cure, so I went alone. Even going alone helped me but it saddened me that my husband gave up.

I attended only two more meetings after that. They were very emotional experiences. When a question was addressed to me, I was so choked up with emotion I could not speak and just cried. I immediately felt the love and compassion of my brothers and sisters in grief and felt no shame. At the next meeting a member handed me a beautiful booklet on faith. Her kind gesture touched me deeply, and I no longer felt alone.

A year later, after trying to go it alone and after terrible experiences with Danny, my husband and I decided that whether there was a magic cure or not, we needed the sup-port of a family group and joined the newly formed Alli-ance.

Community programs affiliated with and sponsored by state departments of mental health can be a source of real help when the professionals are enlightened, compassionate human beings truly concerned with the welfare of mentally ill patients and their families. This is enlightened networking that is not widespread, is not even acceptable by professionals in all areas, but it is growing. The meetings for families sponsored by the aftercare team in Framingham, MA, were shining examples of the good work that is possible. It was out of their work that the concept of this book took root.

> *The weekly meetings* held by the aftercare team were actually education classes and lasted for 12 weeks. We were supplied with publications relating to mental illness. We also had speakers to give us an in-depth idea of mental illness and variations of this disease for which, at present, there is no cure. But there is help.
>
> As a group we came to benefit from the support we received from those who were directing the group as well as from each other. We found great comfort in the fact that we could discuss the problems of our ill family member freely. When the education period came to an end, we were reluctant to disband.
>
> At this time we learned about parents' groups which had formed in a few states in order to support the mentally ill. One father in our education class volunteered to form such a group in Massachusetts. His idea was received most favorably. And so, our Alliance was launched.

Networking through such groups as local chapters of the Alliance for the Mentally Ill provides support to families in many ways. There is the personal, emotional support that makes it possible for parents, sisters, brothers, and other relatives to face each day with a little less heartache, knowing that there are others out there who have the same feelings and problems. There is the practical support that sharing experiences provides—what one parent did under certain circumstances, what another parent did under other circumstances.

These supportive, very personal gatherings are called "sharing and caring" meetings and are held separate from the Alliance business meetings, usually the week after or before. Sharing and caring meetings are exactly what the name implies. Here parents and relatives can talk about their grief, their doubts, their needs. The outpouring of love and caring is extraordinary—and helpful to an extraordinary degree.

> *The Alliance has* been a help for us in so many ways. We work for positive goals that will one day help our loved ones. We enjoy friendship, love, understanding, and humor. We receive advice that comes from experience on how to handle certain situations. Our visits with Danny have become more pleasant because of this. We no longer feel guilty about not allowing our son to live at home, realizing that we are not abandoning him but are actully giving him life, in whatever capacity he is able to grow. We face the inevitable that one day we will be gone from this earth, and he needs the experience to stand on his own with only the help of his support group.
>
> Sometimes, at the support meetings, my mind wanders as I look at the different faces, and I visualize each one during the onset of mental illness in their homes. I see the quiet tears streaming down their cheeks in the middle of the night. I hear their uncontrollable sobs during their moments of solitude in the day and feel their pain, so acute it is indesribable.
>
> The doubts and fears still come and go but on those days help is only a telephone call away, and someone in the Alliance will listen. In sorrow, we have found each other.

Support groups for the families of the mentally ill invariably experience a natural growth toward advocacy, becoming a tool to improve the quality of life and the care given the chronic patients. This not only benefits the afflicted but adds a new dimension to the lives of parents and relatives as they work for positive goals and achievements.

One day I had a telephone call from a young woman who worked in the aftercare and educational program affiliated with the state hospital where my daughter Lora was. She invited me to attend a meeting for parents. I thanked her for thinking of me but said, "No thanks." She was persistent, kind and concerned so I finally said I would go to a meeting to see what it was like.

I was impressed with what I saw and heard. The parents were from every walk of life. They reached out for help, and in their openness and concern, they gave comfort to others. The professionals who ran the group encouraged the parents to speak up but didn't pressure them to do so. They cut in when any one person became long-winded. The group was a revelation to me, and I stayed with it. It was one of the best things I ever did.

From that group I was introduced to and joined our local family support group, the Alliance for the Mentally Ill. I found that there are many thousands of parents across the country who have gone through the same suffering and frustration I had suffered. The Alliance opened my eyes to the vast problems that exist for the long-term mentally ill, as well as to the opportunities to work for improvement. With others in the Alliance I have gone to seminars and workshops for professionals to inform them of the needs of the families of the mentally ill, to tell them to recognize the fact that we can help them in their work. Who knows the ill family member better than the parents?

In a personal sense, the Alliance has become a very important part of my life. Until I joined I had been a confirmed loner, a non-joiner of the first rank. Now I have more friends than I ever had at any one time in my life—kind, giving friends who lighten the burden I had carried alone. I know that at any time I can pick up the phone and talk to somebody who understands. The Alliance has also given me an opportunity to use my skills as a writer and publicist to help educate the public and reeducate the professionals. Other members of the Alliance use their own skills and concerns to the same purposes. We are less frustrated and less guilt-ridden because we understand more and because we are working together to make things better.

The Alliance network, which is a nationwide grass roots organization, is an outstanding example of effective networking. In addition to supporting each other in their desperate hours of need, families and friends are actively working to improve services for the chronically mentally ill, to create new resources, to encourage more research, to improve in all respects the quality of life for those who are ill and unable to speak for themselves.

More and more family members are working with community leaders, informing them about the facts of chronic mental illness—that it is a real, physical disease, not a psychiatric-environmental problem—so that through education the community will become more understanding, and the terrible stigma of mental illness will lessen and eventually disappear.

Families are working with professionals in the field, telling them about the needs of the patients, of the parents, of the sisters and brothers. Except in rare cases, no professional, no average person, can truly understand the emotional and psychological hell that families go through when a son or daughter, a sister or brother, a mother or father becomes chronically mentally ill. Professionals must listen to families in order to understand the depth of the pain, in order to grasp the breadth of the work that needs doing. Book answers studied in college will not suffice.

Family groups are developing mutually beneficial ties with their legislators, working for new bills and regulations that will improve the lot of the mentally ill. Almost all Alliance chapters have a legislative chairman who keeps abreast of state legislation and alerts members when action—such as letter writing and phone calls to legislators—is necessary for the passage of particular bills. The Alliance can also sponsor state legislation or work to have legislators sponsor bills to benefit the mentally ill. In Massachusetts, the state Alliance co-sponsored with a state senator a bill mandating that all hospitals for the chronically mentally ill meet accreditation standards. The families are certain that eventually the bill will pass, even if it has to be reintroduced year after year until it becomes law.

Positive action is possible on many levels. In Massachusetts, to cite that state again as an example, board members of the state Alliance meet regularly with the state mental health commissioner to let him know their concerns and to hear from him what the bureaucracy is planning and doing in various areas of mental health care. It is an educational process on both sides of the table. Not all mental health commissioners are so open-minded but many may be.

In another kind of networking, informal coffee meetings where families invite state representatives and senators within their voting district into their homes have proven very effective in making legislative friends. Neighborly conversation in this kind of friendly setting is an ideal situation for educating the lawmakers about the needs of the mentally ill and giving them the background they require to understand those needs. It is a revelation to learn how little most people know about mental illness, including senators and representatives. Most lawmakers will welcome the opportunity to learn.

> *I found the* coffee klatch setting an ideal way to introduce our local state representative to Alliance voters in his district and to tell him about our concerns. I invited only families within his voting district which, of course, heightened his interest. In this instance that meant six votes for him, plus any ripple effect. He was genuinely interested in what we had to say, and we felt that we had a new friend. In this case it was particularly important because he was a conservative Republican in a predominantly Democratic House—which meant we then had informed contacts on both sides of the aisle.

In addition to the networking that emanates from the families, there is a professional network that is organized and directed by each state. This network, ideally, includes all community workers and programs from psychiatrists to caseworkers, from social clubs to rehabilitation programs. The services offered vary tremendously from state to state, depending upon the concerns and budgets of the various legislative bodies. Federal funds are available to bolster state programs.

In 1974 the National Institute of Mental Health established the Community Support Program to provide guidelines and support to develop the kinds of services and opportunities necessary to maintain the chronically mentally ill in the community. The guidelines use the term "community support system" to describe that network of services. According to the guidelines, a community support system should assure the following essential functions:

1) Identification of the population, whether in hospi-

tals or in the community, and outreach to offer appropriate services.

2) Provision of assistance in applying for income, medical and other entitlements.

3) Provision of quick response 24-hour crisis services in the least restrictive setting possible.

4) Provision of psychosocial rehabilitation services such as goal direction, rehabilitation, evaluation, transitional living arrangements, socialization and vocational rehabilitation.

5) Provision of certain supportive services of indefinite duration, such as living arrangements, work opportunities, and age-appropriate and culturally appropriate daytime and evening activities.

6) Provision of adequate medical and mental health care.

7) Provision of back-up support to family, friends and community members.

8) Involvement of concerned community members in planning, volunteering, and offering housing or work opportunities.

9) Protection of client rights, both in hospitals and in the community.

10) Provision of case management services to assure coordination and continuous availability of appropriate forms of assistance.

These guidelines, as set down by the National Institute of Mental Health, are ideal. Unfortunately, they are not all in place, and even when they are, they too often fall short in effectiveness. It then becomes the responsibility of the families of the long-term mentally ill to monitor the system and its programs to make sure the professionals are on the right road.

For instance, what is "adequate medical care"? Some programs provide an annual physical checkup and consider that enough. But more frequent checkups for the mentally ill are obviously needed. Further, often medical care does not include dental checkups. What "rehabilitation services" are provided? Are they broad in scope or are the patients limited to sheltered workshops that put them in the same classification as the mentally retarded—which the mentally ill are not? Does the back-up support really come through in providing the specific help that is needed for each individual?

These are only some of the areas in which the professional programs can fall short. Families must be constantly vigilant to make sure the help is there when it is needed and that it is forthcoming.

Families in states and regions where there are inadequate programs and little support must not despair. When they bring their own network of parents, relatives, and friends to bear on the problems, outstanding results can be achieved. Even a very small achievement can be considered outstanding when families remember how little was done for the chronically mentally ill only a few short years ago. Every step forward becomes a major achievement. Family advocacy can be a powerful lever politically and legislatively—and it is in the political arena and in the legislative halls where changes and progress come about.

Networking is the magic word. For the families it means emotional support and effective advocacy. For each person involved it becomes an integral part of his or her life. And it can take many different forms.

Writing about my experience with a schizophrenic child has been a great help to me in many ways. First of all, it unleashes my inner turmoil and, somehow, putting it all down on paper helps as I relive the horrible moments and cry it all out.

Then, the making of very dear friends in my writers'

group gives me the feeling of a little more security and the freedom to speak my thoughts, whether positive or negative, without feeling ashamed. We have become very close and know that whatever crisis will come in the future, we are there to comfort and support each other as we impart our own understanding through shared experience.

Another big plus is our ability to laugh. Anyone seeing us going out to lunch together would think we didn't have a care in the world. We can see humor in life and that helps to heal, if only for that day.

This writing experience may have been unique but it can stand as a symbol of what networking is all about.

I found the essence of networking in the committee that came together to write this book.

Our committee was originally made up of four professionals and six family members. The professionals were more progressive in their thinking than their average fellow workers. Though the family members and the professionals frequently argued and disagreed, there was always mutual respect. We had an honest give-and-take relationship. One of the professionals and one of the family members have officially dropped out of the original group, and a second family member feels the need to remain anonymous, but we each still feel close to one another because to some degree we have all been part of an inspiring and fruitful endeavor.

For the family members, who did the actual writing, the book committee became much more than a working arrangement. Though we all belonged to the same chapter of the Alliance for the Mentally Ill and met once a month for the business meeting and once a month for sharing and caring, our friendships were, for the most part, casual. But as we met several times a month to prepare the book—discussing problems, reading about each other's experiences and feelings, opening our hearts and minds to each other—

we became like a family, secure in each other's support and understanding. We became, in fact, a sisterhood that has eased our suffering and enriched our lives.

In addition, working on this book has made it possible for us to speak to "outsiders" openly and without embarrassment.

That, I feel, should be the purpose of all networking— to make the suffering bearable, to nurture compassion and understanding. It can come not only from families and friends but from community support systems, from clinics, from hospital and housing staffs, from therapists and even psychiatrists. But it requires a willingness to communicate, a mind open to suggestion and cooperation, a sincere reaching out by both families and professionals.

Perhaps that sounds like utopia, but it is the goal for which we must strive. We who have worked on this book know it is possible.

Afterword

During the past three years, as we of the Collective have written this book and reached a consensus, as we have worked locally, statewide and nationally to improve conditions for the chronically mentally ill and as we have learned more about the disease itself, some changes have taken place in our thinking and our attitudes.

We started writing in anger, and though much of that anger remains, we now have a greater understanding of the problems. We do not expect overnight solutions—though the apathy, the prejudice, and the bureaucracy that slow down and often prevent solutions keep the anger boiling.

We do not feel quite as angry as we did about "talk therapy." We still think that talk-oriented therapy as a means of improving or lessening symptoms of schizophrenia is not effective and can often be harmful as the major therapeutic approach. But we can now see that talking, in a companionable sense, may be very important to the patient.

Dr. Henry Grunebaum helped clarify that for us when he said, " 'Talking' by itself, in the sense of individual intensive psychoanalytic psychotherapy, may not help schizophrenic patients, but my experience is that it is good for patients to have a counselor to whom they can come and discuss their life, who is not a member of their family but a more impartial outsider. We all use people like that from time to time, and I think schizophrenics are at least entitled to what the rest of us have. If you want to call this kind of supportive counseling "talking therapy," it's okay, but I don't think that psychiatrists and mental health professionals should confine their relationships with patients to dispensing pills without any words at all."

During the writing of this book, and since then, changes have taken place in the condition of the sons and daughters and sisters and brothers we have written about. There have been better periods and darker periods. Overall, their basic situations have not changed to any marked degree. We look for improvement and grasp gratefully at each sign that may mean our children are a little better in some respect. Some of the patients we know, in addition to two of our own children, are now living in community residences, which is a positive step forward. The darker periods return when they regress and have to go back to the hospital, for long or short stays. We keep before us the hopeful theory that as they grow older the symptoms lessen, and they enjoy a measure of "normality."

Notes

1. (Foreword, p. x) GAP (Group for the Advancement of Psychiatry) Committee on the Family. *The Family, the Patient and the Psychiatric Hospital: Toward a New Model.* Report No. 117. New York: Brunner/Mazel, 1985.

2. (Foreword, p. xii) W. R. McFarlane, C. C. Beels, and S. Rosenhack, New Developments in the Family Treatment of the Psychotic Disorders. In: L. Grinspoon (Ed.), *Psychiatry Update: the American Psychiatric Association Annual Review, Volume II.* Washington, DC: The American Psychiatric Association, 1983.

3. (Foreword, p. xiii) John A. Talbott, The Family Psychiatrist. *Psychiatric News,* July 6, 1984.

4. (Chapter 3, p. 32) Statement from Blair Gelbond, coordinator of the sibling group and author of the text in Chapter 3: The use of the terms "sick" and "ill" when referring to a person designated as mentally ill is controversial in many parts of the therapeutic community. While seeming appropriate and nonpejorative to some clinicians, it is to others just the opposite, not accurately describing the person it points to as well as often carrying negative connotations. In this chapter the terms "sick" and "ill" primarily mean dysfunctional in relation to skills of daily living and refer to people having a diagnosis of major mental illness. It should be noted that psychological health and illness are relative terms and always are a matter of degree, affecting every human being in a variety of ways.

5. (Chapter 5, p. 73) The Steadman, Vanderwyst, and Ribner Report appeared in the *American Journal of Psychiatry,* October, 1978.

6. (Chapter 9, p. 123) See Social Security Administration (SSA) Publication No. 05-10029, January 1985 for work credit scale.

7. (Chapter 9, p. 123) SSA Publication No. 05-10052, March 1985.

8. (Chapter 9, p. 123) SSA Publication No. 05-10043, Jan. 1985.

9. (Chapter 9, p. 128) The residences cited are included as examples and are not necessarily recommended by the authors.

10. (Chapter 10, p. 135) Susan M. Hecker tells of her work in the *Psychosocial Rehabilitation Journal*, January 1982.

Affiliates of the National Alliance for the Mentally Ill

The national office of NAMI is at 1901 North Fort Meyer Drive, Suite 500, Arlington, VA 22209 (703-524-7600). In states with state-wide organizations, smaller local affiliates are not listed.

ALABAMA

Birmingham-Tuscaloosa AMI
2061 Fire Pink Ct.
Birmingham, AL 35244
(205) 987-8338

Huntsville Support Alliance for
the Mentally Ill
403 Westburg Avenue
Huntsville, AL 35801
(205) 882-2162

Mobile Family Support Group
4508 Kingsway Ct.
Mobile, AL 36608

Montgomery AMI
1743 Croom Drive
Montgomery, AL 36106

Shoals AMI
2402 Cole
Florence, AL 35630

ALASKA

Alaska AMI
P.O. Box 2543
Fairbanks, AK 99707
(907) 457-3733

ARIZONA

Arizona Alliance for the Mentally
Ill
11810 No. 45th Ave.
Glendale, AZ 85302
(602) 978-3952

ARKANSAS

Help and Hope, Inc.
Arkansas Families and Friends of
the Mentally Ill
4313 W. Markham Hendrix Hall
125
Little Rock, AR 72201
(501) 661-1548

CALIFORNIA

California Alliance for the Mentally Ill
2306 J St. #203
Sacramento, CA 95816
(916) 443-6417

COLORADO

Colorado Alliance for the Mentally Ill
P.O. Box 28008
Lakewood, CO 80228
(303) 321-3104

CONNECTICUT

Connecticut Alliance for the Mentally Ill
284 Battis Road
Hamden, CT 06514
(203) 248-3351

DELAWARE

New Castle Co. AMI
3705 Concord Pike
Wilmington, DE 19803
(302) 478-3060

Sussex County AMI
R.D.#2, Box 177
Georgetown, DE 19947

DISTRICT OF COLUMBIA

Threshold–D.C.
2200 South Dakota Avenue, N.E.
Washington, D.C. 20018
(202) 636-4239

FLORIDA

Florida AMI
c/o Edward H. Gross
P.O. Box A-W
Port Salerno, FL 33492

GEORGIA

Georgia AMI
c/o Vicky Conn
1362 W. Peachtree St.
Atlanta, GA 30309
(404) 636-5735

HAWAII

Hawaii Families and Friends of Schizophrenics, Inc.
P.O. Box 10532
Honolulu, HI 96816
(808) 487-5456

IDAHO

Idaho Alliance for the Mentally Ill
321 Buchanan
American Falls, ID 83211
(208) 336-2346

ILLINOIS

AMI Illinois State Coalition
P.O. Box 863
Glenview, IL 60025
(312) 729-1457

INDIANA

Indiana AMI
P.O. Box 8186
Ft. Wayne, IN 46808
(219) 432-4085

IOWA

Iowa Alliance for the Mentally Ill
509 E. 30th St.
Davenport, IA 52803
(319) 322-5845

KANSAS

Newton Families for Mental
Health
Box 467
Newton, KS 67114
(316) 283-2400

Families for Mental Health, Inc.
P.O. Box 2452
Shawnee Mission, KS 66201
(913) 432-8240

Families for Mental Health Shawnee Co.
4538 NE Meriden Rd.
Topeka, KS 66617
(913) 266-8072

Families for Mental Health
2708-A East Central
Wichita, KS 67214

Wyandotte County Families for
Mental Health
36th at Eaton
Kansas City, KS 66103
(913) 831-9500

KENTUCKY

Kentucky AMI
c/o Kathleen Whipple
145 Constitution Ave.
Lexington, KY 40508
(606) 252-5518

LOUISIANA

Louisiana AMI
1633 Letitia Street
Baton Rouge, LA 70808
(504) 344-2208

MAINE

Maine State AMI, Inc.
P.O. Box 307
Oakland, ME 04963
(207) 547-3639

MARYLAND

AMI of Maryland, Inc.
P.O. Box 336
Kensington, MD 20895
(301) 229-0928

MASSACHUSETTS

AMI of Massachusetts, Inc.
34½ Beacon St.
Boston, MA 02108
(617) 367-8890

MICHIGAN

AMI of Michigan
c/o Peggy Spitzig
17331 Fairfield
Livonia, MI 48152
(313) 421-4825

MINNESOTA

AMI of Minnesota, Inc.
265 Ft. Rd. (W. 7th St.)
St. Paul, MN 55102
(612) 222-2741

MISSISSIPPI

Families and Friends of the Mentally Ill
Rt. 9, Box 385
Hattiesburg, MS 39401
(601) 583-0948

Seeking Help Group for Progress
949 Gooden Cove, Apt. 4
Clarksdale, MS 38614

MISSOURI

Missouri AMI
135 W. Adams, Room G-9
St. Louis, MO 63122
(314) 966-4670

MONTANA

Great Falls AMI
North Central Montana MHC
P.O. Box 3048
Great Falls, MT 59403

FLAME
240 Zimmerman Rd.
Kalispell, MT 59901
(406) 755-1637

Helena AMI
906 Stewart
Helena, MT 59601
(406) 442-7301

A New Beginning for the Mentally Disordered
2405 39th Street
Missoula, MT 59807
(406) 251-2146

Genesis House Inc.
P.O. Box 350
Stevensville, MT 59870

NEBRASKA

Greater Omaha AMI
676 N. 59th Street
Omaha, NE 68132
(402) 556-7659

AMI of Lincoln, Inc.
Lincoln Center Bldg.
215 Centennial Mall South
Lincoln, NE 68508
(402) 467-6285

So. Central NE AMI
Rt. 1, Box 45
Trumbull, NE 68980

Western Nebraska AMI
2280 Pacific Blvd.
Gering, NE 69341
(308) 436-7246

NEVADA

Nevada AMI
3970 Bryarcrest Ct.
Las Vegas, NV 89114
(702) 451-0755

NEW HAMPSHIRE

NAMI in New Hampshire
P.O. Box 544
Peterborough, NH 03458
(603) 924-3069

NEW JERSEY

New Jersey AMI
Box 101, Hoes Lane
Piscataway, NJ 08854
(201) 463-4059

NEW MEXICO

AMI, New Mexico
P.O. Box 876
Santa Fe, NM 87501
(505) 983-2584

NEW YORK

AMI of New York State
42 Elting Avenue
New Paltz, NY 12561
(914) 244-5134

NORTH CAROLINA

North Carolina Alliance for the
  Mentally Ill
P.O. Box 10557
Greensboro, NC 27404
(919) 275-7127

NORTH DAKOTA

REACH
505 19th St. S.W.
Minot, ND 58701
(701) 838-8905

OHIO

Ohio AMI
199 S. Central Ave.
Columbus, OH 43223
(614) 274-7000

OKLAHOMA

Caring Families
1726 NW 49th Street
Lawton, OK 73505

Concerned Citizens for Mental
  Health
5104 N. Francis, Suite B

Oklahoma City, OK 73118
(405) 524-6363

Family Support for Emotional
  Health
c/o Community Support Center
205 East Chestnut
Ponca City, OK 74601

Families Involved-AMI
1719 Glendale Rd.
Sapulpa, OK 74066

Families in Touch
MHA in Tulsa
5 W. 22nd St.
Tulsa, OK 74114
(918) 599-9403

Pontotoc County AMI
P.O. Box 1902
Ada, OK 74820
(405) 332-3645

Tulsa AMI
5710 E. 56th
Tulsa, OK 74135

OREGON

Oregon Alliance for Advocates of
  the Mentally Ill
15693 S. Hidden Rd.
Mulino, OR 97042
(503) 632-3251

PENNSYLVANIA

Pennsylvania AMI
RD4, Box 942
Harrisburg, PA 17112
(717) 599-5998

RHODE ISLAND

New Avenues
RR4, Box 367
N. Scituate, RI 02857

East Bay Advocates
P.O. Box 168
Warren, RI 02885
(401) 245-2386

SOUTH CAROLINA

Greater Charleston AMI
P.O. Box 32084
Charleston, SC 29407-2538
(803) 795-4600

SOUTH DAKOTA

Northeastern MHC Family Support Group
Box 550
Aberdeen, SD 57401
(605) 225-1010

Brookings AMI
1323 5th St.
Brookings, SD 57006
(605) 692-5673

Sioux Falls AMI
2201 W. 37th Street
Sioux Falls, SD 57105

TENNESSEE

Tennessee AMI
416 E. Thompson La.
Nashville, TN 37211
(615) 361-7950 or 7858

TEXAS

Texas AMI
P.O. Box 50434

Austin, TX 78759
(512) 327-4253

UTAH

Utah AMI
156 Westminster Ave.
Salt Lake City, UT 84115
(801) 484-3314

VERMONT

AMI Vermont
9 Andrews Avenue
So. Burlington, VT 05401
(802) 655-2525

VIRGINIA

Virginia AMI
4010 W. Franklin St.
Richmond, VA 23221
(804) 358-6980

WASHINGTON

AMI of Washington State
12920 N.E. 14th Street
Vancouver, WA 98684
(206) 892-6323

WEST VIRGINIA

Charleston AMI
5453 Kingswood Lane
Charleston, WV 25313
(304) 776-2666

AMI of Eastern Panhandle
404 Edgemont Terrace
Martinsburg, WV 25401
(304) 263-9847

Huntington Area AMI
208 12th Avenue

Huntington, WV 25701
(304) 523-3385

South Branch Valley AMI
Rt. 2, Box 24
Moorefield, WV 26836
(304) 434-2443

WISCONSIN

AMI of Wisconsin, Inc.
1245 E. Washington Ave.
Suite 212
Madison, WI 53703
(608) 257-5888

WYOMING

Wyoming AMI
1123 Beaumont Dr.
Casper, WY 82601
(307) 234-4775

CANADA

Association of Relatives &
  Friends of the Mentally and
  Emotionally Ill
P.O. Box 322, Snowdon Branch
Montreal, Quebec H3X 3T6
(514) 937-5351

PUERTO RICO

Asociacion Familiares y Voluntar-
  ios Pro-Participantes Centro
  Psicosacirol de Baya mon
Antiguo Hosp. Ruis Soler
Carr. #2
Bayamon, Puerto Rico 00619

VIRGIN ISLANDS

St. Croix Concerned Citizens for
  Mental Health, Inc.
P.O. Box 937 Kings Hill
St. Croix, VI 00850

73560

DATE DUE

NOV 25 '87			

DEMCO 38-297